Watch and See

Only look down to lift up your gems of understanding your paw so you can look up and share them with another.

2 Corinthians 4:17

Bishop Marcus A. Johnson, Sr.

Watch and See

A Journey Into the Revelation
of the Miraculous

Marcus A. Johnson, Sr.

Copyright © 2017 by Marcus A. Johnson, Sr. Ministries, Inc.

Library of Congress Control Number: 2017916498
ISBN: Hardcover 978-1-5434-6126-8
Softcover 978-1-5434-6127-5
eBook 978-1-5434-6128-2

All rights reserved. No part of this book may be reproduced or transmitted in any form or by any means, electronic or mechanical, including photocopying, recording, or by any information storage and retrieval system, without permission in writing from the copyright owner.

KJV
Scripture quotations marked KJV are from the Holy Bible, King James Version (Authorized Version). First published in 1611. Quoted from the KJV Classic Reference Bible, Copyright © 1983 by The Zondervan Corporation.

NKJV
Scripture quotations marked NKJV are taken from the New King James Version. Copyright © 1982 by Thomas Nelson, Inc. Used by permission. All rights reserved.

Any people depicted in stock imagery provided by Thinkstock are models, and such images are being used for illustrative purposes only.
Certain stock imagery © Thinkstock.

Print information available on the last page.

Rev. date: 12/27/2017

To order additional copies of this book, contact:
Xlibris
1-888-795-4274
www.Xlibris.com
Orders@Xlibris.com
769656

CONTENTS

Preface ix
Foreword xi

Chapter 1   I want a testimony 1
Chapter 2   The gap 7
Chapter 3   What time is it? 17
Chapter 4   A rainbow in the falls 27
Chapter 5   The enemy in me (codependency) 37
Chapter 6   On a walk with God 43
Chapter 7   A strange place to be 47
Chapter 8   Right on the verge 51
Chapter 9   A way of escape 55
Chapter 10   God is waiting for the perfect moment 61
Chapter 11   Finding the new normal 81
Chapter 12   My miracle son 87
Chapter 13   There is laughter in my pain 93
Chapter 14   Come over to this side of Jordan 97

Epilogue   I'm committed to finish the work 103
Acknowledgments 105
About the Author 107

Dedications

I would like to dedicate this work to several people to
whom I believe I have been called to uplift
when I share my journey and what I've learned along the way.
This book is dedicated to all:
who struggle with any kind of affliction or
captivity that appears to have no end;
care providers, family members, and friends to
someone suffering afflictions and hardships;
survivors and bereaved who are left to make sense
out of great loss with much pain;
spiritual leaders called to lead people through and beyond captivity.
Watch and See is for you.
As you read this book, you will discover that all
afflictions are a type of captivity and are real.
Yet, God has a pathway through these struggles
that leads to a place of deliverance,
enlightenment, empowerment, and purpose for ministry.
Dear reader, God has a plan.
Watch and See

Preface

Watch and See has been a project in my spirit since 1989, and it has been a challenge for me to bring it to fruition as I have been waiting for clarity and the time to release this work. Knowing that I am to author many books, it has been difficult to know the inception and terminus of book one—so that it would, in fact, be a completed work.

Often, as a pastor I would find the compulsion to write this book as I was preaching a sermon. Even as I would fly internationally and ascend into the clouds, there again the motivation to write would be stirred. It was as if the essence of this book was somehow bound up within a higher altitude accessible only while I was flying and in conversation with God. In 2011, my passion to write was rekindled, and I began this work entitled *Watch and See.*

Watch and See speaks of God's twofold mandate to me, first, to assess the conditions and circumstances that surround and challenge me. Secondly, I am to observe the miracle He is going to build out of its ruins.

Upon Moses' exodus out of Egypt, he was blocked by the Red Sea. The Egyptian pursuers signaled impending danger for the Israelites who were terrified. Moses looked up, as if to say to God, "what am I supposed to do?"

"And Moses said unto the people, Fear ye not, stand still, and see the salvation of the Lord, which he will shew to you to day: for the Egyptians whom ye have seen to day, ye shall see them again no more for ever." Exodus 14:13 (KJV)

The stand still commandment is interpreted as watch, observe, assess, and accept that what you are faced with is humanly impossible to resolve. Stand still, or watch, there is a definite enemy that is seeking to destroy you. Stand still, or watch, there is a body of water that you cannot cross. It has blocked you from moving forward. Stand still Moses, or watch Moses, you are surrounded with a nation of people who have trusted you to lead them into safety. There is nothing you can do to resolve this dilemma. And God said, "...stand still, and see..." God spoke this same command to me during my second out of body experience when

I was pronounced dead. Therefore, I am compelled to entitle this work, *Watch and See*.

"Stand still, and see the salvation of the Lord, which He will accomplish for you today." Exodus 14:13 (NKJV)

Watch and See is my personal story—the process of standing still and watching one dilemma after the other threaten my life. God, in the midst of my ruins, has miraculously enabled me to overcome each obstacle. Like Israel, I too can say "This is the Lord's doing; It is marvelous in our eyes." Psalm 118:23 (KJV)

Israel crossed the Red Sea, and looked back confidently, realizing that their Egyptian pursuers had been drowned. My testimony is of a faith journey where I had to see in the spirit before I could see in the natural.

Therefore, it is the aim of *Watch and See* to address people in various situations to consider your impossibilities and realize, "With men this is impossible; but with God all things are possible." Matthew 19:26 (KJV)

In the following pages, you will read my testimony of miraculous healing which unfolded between 1983 and 1990. This book is not written chronologically. Instead, I have chosen to convey my testimony thematically so that each reader will be able to identify and apply the principles I learned during my seven year journey.

It is my prayer that as you read my testimony, your faith will be strengthened. I believe that you will have a testimony as well—God you opened my Red Sea allowing me to cross on dry ground; God you closed my sea drowning my pursuers. I pray that as you read, you will be inspired to overcome your dilemma despite its magnitude. *Watch and See*.

Foreword

On behalf of my father, the late Dr. Elijah Saunders, congratulations are extended to Bishop Marcus A. Johnson, Sr. He has put his extraordinary testimony into written form for the world to *Watch and See* that miracles still happen. During the period of Bishop Johnson's journey toward recovery from his accident, my father superintended his medical treatment to ensure that he was provided with the best of care and medical guidance. From a medical standpoint, my father attested to Bishop Marcus' encounters, with both near death and actual death, during his long road to recovery. He would often shake his head in amazement, testifying that only by God's power is Bishop Marcus alive and able to testify with all of his faculties. Dr. Saunders would further attest that while modern medicine can explain some things, experiences such as what he witnessed in the case of Bishop Marcus can only be explained by, and attributed to, God and God alone. On behalf of the late Dr. Elijah Saunders and the innumerable cloud of witnesses in Heaven (including my mother), you are challenged, Bishop Marcus, to tell the whole world that faith and medicine are compatible, not in opposition, in the performance of miracles.

—The Late Dr. Elijah Saunders, MD, FACC, FACP, FAHA, FASH, Professor of Medicine and Head of the Section of Hypertension in the University of Maryland School of Medicine, Division of Cardiovascular Medicine (submitted by his daughter, Dr. Donna Saunders)

MARCUS A. JOHNSON, SR.

I have had the privilege of knowing Bishop Marcus A. Johnson, Sr., all of my life and have, within that time, only known him to be a dedicated and upright servant of the Lord. I have teased, when addressing his congregation with my childhood perception, that Bishop Marcus was 'born saved'. I don't know a time in his life when he was not giving glory, honor, and praise to God. It makes biblical sense, in my view, that God would choose this vessel to experience the unexpected, enigmatic, yet ultimately miraculous testimony (comparable to that of Job). The accident in 1983 catapulted Bishop Marcus into his destiny as a firsthand witness of the supernatural, resurrection power of God. In reading *Watch and See*, you are sure to witness in the 21st Century yet another journey of faith, involving the joy of salvation, combined with the agony of loss, grief, and painful perplexity, followed by refreshing and renewal that comes with restoration and recovery. These describe the multiple dimensions of a life committed to glorify God, no matter the cost. Such is the life of Bishop Marcus A. Johnson, Sr. *Watch and See!*

—Dr. Donna Saunders, Psychologist and CEO, Guide Global Health Initiatives

Chapter 1

I WANT A TESTIMONY

> "And when Abram was ninety years old and nine, the Lord appeared to Abram, and said unto him, I am the Almighty God; walk before me, and be thou perfect. And I will make my covenant between me and thee, and will multiply thee exceedingly. And Abram fell on his face: and God talked with him saying, As for me, behold, my covenant is with thee, and thou shall be a father of many nations. Neither shall thy name any more be called Abram, but thy name shall be Abraham; for a father of many nations have I made thee. And I will make thee exceeding fruitful, and I will make nations of thee, and kings shall come out of thee."
> *Genesis 17:1-6 (KJV)*

> "And they overcame him by the blood of the Lamb, and by the word of their testimony; and they loved not their lives unto the death."
> *Revelation 12:11 (KJV)*

These scripture passages speak of God foreordaining our destiny. God works through process. He will give us a word of promise before its manifestation. This repeat method—God promising us and God working through process—is relevant to this book, *Watch and See*.

At the age of twelve, I was attending a week night worship service at my local church, First United Church of Jesus Christ Apostolic. A young sister at the church (named Helen Dyson and fondly known as Nookie), had been in a bad car accident, and she had come back to the church after recovering. In that service, I remember her testifying about what the Lord had done; how God had preserved her and kept her. And the church was so blessed, and there was such a rapturous encounter with God—ecstatic worship and praise flowed from the mouths of the saints seemingly up to the gates of Heaven—as a result of her testimony.

As a child, I didn't think that I had a testimony to offer unto the Lord that would bring Him glory and that would create such a joyous experience among the people of God on a higher scale. And for some strange reason, beyond my childhood understanding, I wanted to be able to praise God. I became depressed in that service. I was so young and didn't quite understand my feelings, in general, or for God, but there was a deep longing in my heart for something bigger than I had experienced before.

As I was leaving the sanctuary, I entered the hallway and crossed paths with one of the deacons. Even now, as I am writing this about deceased Deacon Elmer Pace, I can recall that he had a uniquely beautiful singing voice. He stopped me right there in the hallway and asked, "young man why are you so sad in your countenance?"

I said to him, "Because I don't have a testimony to be able to bless the name of the Lord."

I remember that we could still hear the residual praise and worship of the saints, in the sanctuary, still praising God for the testimony that the sister had shared in the service.

And Deacon Pace cautioned me, "Young man, be careful what you ask God for."

I replied, "But I want a testimony."

He said, "Are you sure that you want a testimony?"

I replied with tears streaming down my face, "Yes sir."

He said, "Ok son, then I'm going to pray for you that God will give you a testimony."

He laid his hands on my head and he began to pray aloud. I heard him ask God to give me a testimony that would be a tremendous blessing to the body of Christ and that my testimony would bring glory to God's name. He prayed, and his prayer reached the very empty spot where my heart was longing.

As he prayed, I began to fall, and I knew that I was experiencing God as my arms and legs gave way to the floor. There I lay in the lobby under the power of the Holy Spirit.

What made this experience so amazing is that the lobby tiles were placed in a black and red arrangement. When I got up from the floor, I realized for the first time that there was a pattern in the tile that formed a cross at the very site where the deacon had prayed. I fell directly onto the impression of the cross that was embedded in the tiled floor.

It is evident to me as I am writing this that from the ages of seven to twelve, I like so many other congregants had repeatedly passed over the spot marked with the cross in the hallway. However, I was blessed to literally lay, or to figuratively hang upon it. I had never realized that beneath the surface of the floor's design was the opportunity to discover my spiritual cross—my testimony. Just as Jesus made the ultimate sacrifice, at the appointed time, He was nailed to the cross as it lay upon the ground. For me, my cross was foreshadowed by the design on the tile floor; through my sacrifice of worship, my testimony, foreordained from the foundation of the world, would unfold. I had to descend into hurt, into pain, into death to carry my cross which was embedded in the tiles under my feet. Just as God had promised Abraham the ground wherever his feet traveled so had He destined my steps.

Certainly, then at the age of twelve, I didn't understand the significance or meaning of this moment. Decades later, I can see that God was foreshadowing my destiny. He was literally giving me the desire to be a praise unto Him through my testimony. God was preordaining my destiny in the midst of witnesses. He was making a covenant with me that He would be my deliverer in times of trouble and great distress. He was engrafting me into the cross—the concurrent symbol of suffering and life. Indeed, this testimony would be a life-giving sacrifice. It was going to require death. But oh, in the death there would be a resurrection.

It's amazing how God will manifest His Will through foreshadowing and often He will allow years and years of dormancy before the fullness of His Will is manifested.

That moment will forever be present with me as it was the harbinger of my testimony that began just fourteen years later on February 22, 1983.

Still, there was another foreshadowing experience and encounter. At the age of twenty, I desired to be married. My wife, Ronaé Angela Banks, was my girlfriend at the time. I remember speaking with the late Chief Apostle Monroe R. Saunders, Sr., D.Min., who was my Senior Pastor, Presiding Bishop, and father in the gospel. I asked him to provide us with more premarital counseling, which was then beyond his normal practice due to the size of his ministry. Being led of the Holy Spirit, Bishop Saunders recommended that I counsel with a seasoned saint in the church, a very deeply spiritual mother by the name of Reverend Shirley Carrington (Mother Carrington).

I approached Mother Carrington with my request and she invited me to her home for counseling sessions. She would go on to meet with me for six months prior to our wedding. I would go to her home at least once a month in the evening. Upon entering her home, I greeted her husband and her daughter. Following a brief salutation, I would go into the basement where Mother Carrington was always waiting to begin with prayer.

I'm not sure what I anticipated that these sessions would entail, but God had a greater purpose that was rooted in prayer. Mother Carrington would play worship music that would invite the presence of God into the room as we prayed. I recall that these encounters with God were always very sobering.

In one of our sessions, Mother Carrington began to prophesy aloud to me. She said, "God is going to use you in a great way." She prophesied about our wedding and how Ronaé and I would entertain such a great crowd on that day. She told me that we would be blessed to receive so many gifts. Just six months later, all the details that she prophesied about the wedding happened.

It was amazing that when I arrived at the church on our wedding day, June 3, 1978, there was no one there except my brothers and a few church members. I remember feeling disappointed because of my longstanding history with my church family and because I trusted the God in Mother Carrington. She was known for speaking what the Lord had said through prophecy. However, because of the horrendous rainstorm on that day, the wedding was delayed by more than an hour. The bridal party arrived so late. But when my bride Ronaé arrived, the church was packed from the main floor to the balcony.

Even now, as I reflect upon our wedding day, I can see that God was teaching me through a process. Sometimes what God has promised may not appear to be working out, but you've got to wait for it because process takes and uses time.

In Mother Carrington's basement, the true essence of her prophecy related to my testimony. She said, "And God is going to bless your wife and your children to stand with you in ministry." I remember pondering, "what ministry?" I then concluded these words must mean the choirs that I directed. At the age of twenty-one, those words resounded in my spirit. "Your wife and your children will stand with you in ministry."

Well, as God would have it, no different than in the case of Abram, who was renamed Abraham, the Lord was telling me in advance that despite the challenges I would face, I would survive to see the fulfillment of His promises. Little did I know, at that time, that a fatal accident awaited me just five years later. It is critical to note that at the time of the accident, my wife and I had only one child. But God had promised me children. Despite what the doctors would later diagnose, despite the dreadful prognoses and the doubts that cast a dark shadow on any hope of recovery, I would survive the crises. I would survive the accident, the challenges, the surgeries, the financial devastation, and the setbacks because God promised that I would emerge as a husband to my wife and a father to my **CHILDREN**. In the same way that God changed Abram's name to prepare him for his new role as father, God changed my role from local youth choir director, to national youth choir director, to minister, to youth pastor, to elder, to senior pastor, and then to bishop over a span of thirty-three years. Just as God promised Abraham that he would father many, over this time span, spiritually, I am a father to many **CHILDREN** who stand in ministry with me throughout this region and abroad.

WATCH and SEE

Honestly, I had no clue what the word ministry meant, and I had no appreciation for the scope of the testimony that God would give me. In this same way, it was imperceptible to me at the age of twelve how the course of my destiny forever would be changed as Deacon Elmer Pace laid his hands on me and prayed for me to receive years earlier.

But the scripture in Romans is correct, "For we do not know what we should pray for as we ought, but the Spirit Himself makes intercession for us with groanings which cannot be uttered." Romans 8:26 (NKJV)

Often the Spirit will pray on our behalf, overriding our limited vocabulary and intellectual understanding. The Holy Spirit will find the exact words that translate to God what our spirits really desire deep within us—and deep calleth unto deep, and the deep in God called unto the deep that was within my spirit, calling for a testimony that would bring glory to the body of Christ. This would minister to God and bring Him glory.

It was the deep calling unto deep that would empower Deacon Pace to pray as I fell onto the cross embedded in the tiled floor. It was the deep calling unto deep in Bishop Saunders when he directed me to Mother Carrington. It was the deep calling unto deep that would pull out of Mother Carrington prophetic sayings that I would need to hold onto as a promise. I would hold onto them just as childless Abraham held onto the promise that he would be a father to many. I held onto the words of promise that I would come forth and that my wife and children would also survive the difficulty—my marriage, my daughter, and then after my healing, a biological son of promise would emerge and many spiritual children through my ministry would come forth also. Not only would we all survive, but we would stand together as a couple, family, church family, community, and internationally through global missions.

To this day, I don't believe that the full essence of this word has come to its completion because the ministry that God has ordained is still unfolding. Thus, the impetus for this opening chapter is to crystalize the truth that "Being confident of this very thing, that he which hath begun a good work in you will perform it until the day of Jesus Christ." Philippians 1:6 (KJV)

Words of Wisdom to Readers

Come hell or high water, God will bring to pass what He has promised. And He will always promise it before the challenge. Therefore, when we are challenged, we are to hold onto the promise firmly throughout the process. Don't let go. And what He has promised, God will bring it to pass. What God starts, He will finish.

Ultimately, we are required to walk by faith to see the unseen fulfillment of God's promise in our blessed destiny as we look beyond the contradictions of our now!

"Watch and See."

> "God is not a man, that he should lie; neither the son of man, that he should repent: hath he said, and shall he not do it? or hath he spoken, and shall he not make it good?" Numbers 23:19 (KJV)

> "And Moses said unto the people, Fear ye not, stand still, and see the salvation of the Lord, which he will shew to you to day: for the Egyptians whom ye have seen to day, ye shall see them again no more for ever." Exodus 14:13 (KJV)

Chapter 2

THE GAP

> "In the beginning God created the Heaven and the earth. And the earth was without form, and void; and darkness was upon the face of the deep. And the Spirit of God moved upon the face of the waters."
> Genesis 1:1-2 (KJV)

Many theologians disagree on the interpretation of the two opening verses of the Bible.

Verse one reads, "In the beginning God created the Heaven and the earth." And then verse two, "And the earth was without form, and void; and darkness was upon the face of the deep. And the Spirit of God moved upon the face of the waters."

For some scholars, verse one merely explains the process God evoked as Creator, as He produced the masterpiece we know as earth. Then verse two begins the detailed explanation of all God created in the earth.

Yet, other theologians highlight a stark difference in the function of these two verses. In this view, verse one is a summary which captures the total completed work of God, creating Heaven and the earth. And then verse two describes the re-creation of earth. But why you ask would the earth created in verse one need to be re-created in verse two? Theologians taking this perspective believe in the "Gap Theory" that literally there is a gap between God's initial creation of the earth in verse one and His subsequent re-creation of the earth in verse two.

MARCUS A. JOHNSON, SR.

Gap Theory in creationism considers Isaiah 14:12[1] and Revelation 12:9[2] which describes the Satan led revolt in Heaven, resulting in the loss of one-third of the angelic host (known as the fallen angels). Ultimately, Satan and the fallen angels were cast out of Heaven, for their rebellion against God, into the earth. Once inhabitants of the earth, this dark envoy decimated and destroyed the first masterpiece (earth).

Within this context, I will focus on verse two. "And the earth was without form, and void; and darkness was upon the face of the deep."

I ascribe to this theological perspective and see the Gap Theory as a remarkable explanation of how we can understand God's miraculous re-creation of the earth. As I delve a bit deeper, I posit that we all have a "gap" in our lives. This is a season, a time, a moment where good days were interrupted by unexpected bad days; and we go from the highest mountaintop to the lowest point of the valley. A theological world view causes Christians to trust God to take the void and darkness of the valley and re-create us anew.

I invite you to follow along intently as I roll back the clock to a gap in my life, which occurred on February 22, 1983 at 7:15pm.

Let's actually rewind the clock a bit further to about a week prior. My family was in full celebration mode preparing for my younger brother (by nearly six years) Samuel's wedding. My wife, parents, sister, and two younger brothers were discussing our remaining to do's leading up to the wedding on that coming Saturday. And then the phone rang.

I remember with great excitement and glee answering the phone call. This call was literally the pin that burst our celebration bubble. Sadly, my brother Samuel (whom we affectionately call "Sam") was on the other line. He was calling from the hospital with shockingly disturbing news. His father-in-law to be, the bride's dad, was dead.

Sam's voice was breaking on the phone.

He kept asking me, "Marcus, what am I supposed to do?"

To any big brothers or big sisters reading, we are supposed to have all of the answers. We are supposed to protect our younger siblings. Sadly, in that moment, I had nothing to offer. I remember gesturing to my family to quiet down as I tried to listen and understand the information that Sam was relaying to me.

I asked, "Sam, what happened?"

---

[1] How art thou fallen from Heaven, O Lucifer, son of the morning! how art thou cut down to the ground, which didst weaken the nations! (King James Version)

[2] And the great dragon was cast out, that old serpent, called the Devil, and Satan, which deceiveth the whole world: he was cast out into the earth, and his angels were cast out with him. (King James Version)

WATCH and SEE

It turns out that Sam's father-in-law was hospitalized for about seven days, but we all expected him to be discharged. The plan was that he would recuperate sufficiently at home while the wedding preparations continued. It was expected that on the wedding day, the bride's father would be well enough to walk his youngest daughter down the aisle.

However, there were unexpected complications. His condition worsened, and he died. But just before departing, the bride's father's dying request to his wife was that my sister-in-law to be and Sam were to go forward with the wedding as planned. He told them he was going to Heaven to be with the Lord. He told them he did not want the wedding to be cancelled or postponed.

And just like that, he was gone.

Sam was talking.

I was listening.

Sam was crying.

I could feel my heart pounding in my ears.

"Marcus, he's dead," Sam breathed through the phone.

This truth was echoing throughout my brain, and I just didn't know what to say.

"Marcus, what am I supposed to do?"

I gasped for air, but it was as if there was no more air in the room. I inhaled and exhaled slowly. I prayed and asked God to give me words of comfort and direction for my brother Sam.

Within a few days, the decision was made to honor the request of the deceased. The wedding would go on as planned. By the miraculous hand of God, we pulled ourselves together. We attended the final wedding rehearsal on Thursday as the bride's mother and siblings made the funeral arrangements. On Saturday, we were all standing at the altar in the wedding. By the grace of God, the wedding went on without a hitch. There were close to 700 guests in attendance. The onlookers watched a beautiful grieving bride walk down the long aisle, escorted by her older brother instead of her father.

At that time, I was the church youth leader and choir director. In the Sunday worship service, I led the 200 plus voice youth choir (which would have included my brother and sister-in-law at any other time) in song. The choir ministered so greatly and there was a comradery among the youth. We felt uplifted as we prepared for the funeral on Monday night.

Finally, on Monday, the bride, her family, and now my brother, walked down the same church aisle, arm and arm, in the funeral procession. The then First United Church of Jesus Christ Apostolic was filled. Hundreds of mourners, many of whom attended the wedding on Saturday, were packed into the same church to bid farewell to a Christian soldier. God's will was done and many souls were saved and revived in that funeral service.

MARCUS A. JOHNSON, SR.

On Tuesday morning, February 22, I was back at work. I was the Assistant Manager of Kinney Shoes located in Westview Mall (Baltimore County, Maryland). I could not take time off to attend the burial even though I wanted to be there so badly. Instead, that afternoon, after the burial my late grandmother Annabelle (affectionately called "Dear") and my Aunt Jeanette (affectionately known as "Jenny") came to the store. They told me about the burial and how well Sam and his new bride were doing.

I remember feeling extremely relieved. I rejoiced that within seven days God had performed quite a miracle in getting everyone involved (in the wedding and funeral) through quite an impossible ordeal. Everything was accomplished with such excellence and grace.

It was now early evening, about 6:00pm when a seasoned saint entered my store. We immediately began discussing the things of God and the store sale. She quickly became my ideal customer. She was interested in multiple items and, as a result, I was expecting a large commission.

It seemed as if things were turning back around. I could see the sun rising through the clouds. I was already in great spirits because of the good report concerning the burial. The worst was over. Now, God sent me a customer who wanted seven pairs of shoes. She was even looking at accessories, too. Then I could barely believe my ears. She was interested in buying her eighth pair of shoes. Because the particular shoes were discontinued stock, I had to leave the floor and retrieve them from a designated section in the back of the stockroom. Off I went. I began to sing one of my favorite hymns.

> *Blessed assurance, Jesus is mine,*
> *O what a foretaste of glory divine.*
> *Heir of salvation, purchase of God,*
> *Born of His Spirit, washed in His blood.*
>
> *This is my story, this is my song,*
> *Praising my Savior all the day long.*
> *This is my story, this is my song,*
> *Praising my Savior all the day long.*

Wait a minute. I stopped and recalled a construction crew had been in the stockroom that week repairing the ceiling of the store. Although they were gone for the day, they had left a three-foot pallet of sheetrock directly in front of the shelf I needed to access. Our store staff seldom sold shoes retrieved from this area. However, the sheetrock was blocking my ability to easily get to the shoe shelf.

Literally, there were two stacks of sheetrock on the pallet: one stack was laid horizontally on the pallet and was the approximate height of my waist; and

WATCH and SEE

the second stack was leaning horizontally against the shoe shelves, atop the first stack. I'm 5 ft. 10 in. tall and at that time, I weighed about 160 lbs. I needed to get the eighth pair of shoes for my waiting customer, so I attempted to reach over the second stack of sheetrock.

I remember wondering why the construction men would leave the second stack of sheetrock in the work area, and also, why it was not tied down or buckled in any way.

So, I tried to carefully reach over the sheetrock and not disturb the angle at which it was leaning on the shelves. I didn't want to cause the sheetrock to fall and break.

I continued to sing the chorus of the hymn:

This is my story, this is my song,
Praising my Savior all the day long.

On February 22, 1983 at 7:14pm I didn't know how much sheetrock weighed. I reached over the sheetrock and grabbed the intended shoe box, accidentally touching the sheetrock panel closest to me. It tilted towards me. I panicked. I tried pushing it back into place. But then, I felt its weight. I immediately planted my feet on the waxed tile floor, but I was wearing dress shoes. The floor was providing no traction. I braced my right hip up against the sheetrock that was leaning and now falling. I frantically tried to push the falling sheetrock back into place, but gravity was winning. The sheetrock was falling. I couldn't get any grip to anchor myself. My head hit the metal bar on the display cart located right behind me and I fell to the tile floor. The sheetrock was too heavy. It was falling hard upon me. It was so heavy on my body. At 7:15pm time stopped. There was a gap.

In slow motion, I watched each sheet fall in succession on top of me. The twenty-four sheets each weighed 100 lbs. The noise was deafening. I saw the dust and debris swirling in the air like a thick smoke. I entered a divine zone between time and eternity. I felt no pain. I was shocked and fully aware of what had happened. Lying there on my back, I was facing the back cinder block wall of the store. I watched the wall open up like curtains on an auditorium stage. The open wall revealed a tunnel, and it was flooded with light. It was as though my body unzipped itself and released my spirit which was drawn as if by a magnet into the tunnel. I (my spirit) was being pulled into the light. I was moving faster than I had ever flown in an airplane. And I felt death as an ominous force pushing me in the tunnel, towards the light, to the other side of life, Heaven. Yet, the brighter the light became, I was aware that death's push was weakening. And the closer I came to the light, the more I could tolerate looking into the light. Different from my earth experience, as I had shielded my eyes on bright summer mornings from the sun, here in the tunnel, I peered into the light with ease. When I reached the end of the tunnel, I stepped out into the brightest, cleanest, purest light I have ever experienced. Over there, I didn't just see the light, I felt the light. I looked down and saw a beautiful crystal clear river. It was simply breathtaking. At the bottom of the river, instead of regular stones, there were glittering jewels. I saw jaspers, rubies, crystals, and diamonds just glistening and sparkling.

I lifted my eyes to look out in front of me and saw the green pastures described in Psalm 23:2.[3] There was a massive field of green grass. It was perfectly manicured. I saw the blades of grass swaying in the breeze. It was as if each blade was so full of life. It was a rich green and lush pasture. In the farthest distance, I saw the mountain of God. As I continued to stare, I could look through the mountain, and there was an innumerable company of saints celebrating. They were rejoicing as they anticipated receiving me into the City.

I knew exactly where I was. I had passed through the valley of the shadow of death and entered the garden, outside of the city called Heaven.

Standing behind an imperial wrought iron gate, in front of many saints were my grandfather, Samuel Johnson, my great Uncle, Emmett Wood, and Deacon McNeil Brockington. I knew they were at the gate, waiting ecstatically to receive me.

Harmonious with the light I felt the crystal river at my feet. I saw the green pasture in front of me, and the mountain in the distance. Then I heard a voice incomparable to any other voice. It was God. He was speaking to me. His voice was authoritative but reassuring. His voice was commanding but clear. His voice was Holy, but I was not afraid. His voice enveloped my spirit. God was everywhere.

---

[3] "He maketh me to lie down in green pastures: he leadeth me beside the still waters."(King James Version)

I was breathing the breath of God, and like Adam with the breath of life, I was a living soul.[4] I was raptured into His divine presence. It was the zenith and apex of joy and eternal ecstasy.

"MARCUS AARON JOHNSON, YOU ARE GOING TO LIVE. AND WHEN YOU GET BACK TELL EVERYONE THAT HEAVEN IS A REAL PLACE."

God called my name.

He was speaking directly to me.

Yet, as I listened, He said "when you get back."

This disappointed me because I did not want to leave.

I knew instantly what He was saying. I was going back to earth.

"AND WHEN YOU GET IN TROUBLE CALL FOR HELP."

I thought of the scripture, "For whosoever shall call upon the name of the Lord shall be saved." Romans 10:13 (KJV)

But I didn't want to go back to earth. In a last desperate attempt, I proceeded to walk on the river. I had the awareness to know that I could walk on the water. I thought, if I could get to the gate of the City, I could plead with God not to send me back. I thought if I could get closer, where the saints were gathered, God would grant me my heart's desire to stay.

Nevertheless, God in His sovereignty pushed my spirit back. This time, I faced the light and moved backwards through the tunnel (Heaven was in front of me and earth was behind me). In the tunnel the bright light became less bright as I traveled back to earth. The light became dim and then gray.

Suddenly, I was jolted back into my body.

I lay there under the sheetrock.

Immediately, I heard a man yelling, "He's back. I got a pulse."

Then for the first time in my life, I felt an unexplainable, excruciating pain. I cannot use words to describe the pain I felt. As I laid there on the floor, I realized I had left Heaven, my ultimate home, to return to the earth. I felt as if I was in a nightmare.

Lying in that position I was fully conscious. My mind was flooded with every thought imaginable. I understood that I, Marcus, physically fit, healthy, sound in soul and spirit, was changed. And with the physical pain, I felt another acute pain, and it was emotional. Life as I knew it was different. I was hurting in my back, my legs, my hips, and my arms. It felt like my heart was broken and I was at the lowest point of my existence. My life was void and dark. But the Spirit of God moved across my dark waters. He would use a gap of seven years to re-create me into a new vessel with a miraculous testimony.

---

[4] "And the Lord God formed man of the dust of the ground, and breathed into his nostrils the breath of life; and man became a living soul." Genesis 2:7 (KJV)

"Watch and See!"

Words of Wisdom to Readers

The Gap Theory in and of itself is a powerful discovery of how God works. It presupposes that there was an original design that had been severely damaged. Yet, God will use the process of gap seasons in our lives to address damages. God, the ultimate creator, will allow things to be redone. This results in a re-creation. And this truth is reassuring, knowing that God intends to reassemble and restore the broken pieces when we trust in Him.

There are four key teaching points that I want to make at the end of this chapter. First, let's understand that God's original intent can never be frustrated or thwarted. Clearly, Gap Theory demonstrates that God's plan from the beginning consists of a Heaven and an earth. And when His creation is damaged by sin or circumstances, God in His infinite wisdom prepares a redo. God will always preserve His original intent.[5] This is evident as God responds to the fall of the first Adam by sending the second Adam, in the man Jesus Christ. Jesus, our Redeemer, through his sacrificial death on the cross, offers redemption to all of us who believe.[6] He re-creates us as new creatures. In our redeemed state, we satisfy God's original intent and purpose for man, which is to have dominion over the earth.[7]

Second, it is vitally important to recognize that when we worship God following a storm, we are exhibiting prophetic worship in and through our seasons of gaps. I practiced prophetic worship as I sang *Blessed Assurance,* celebrating my family's overcoming the challenges that occurred, surviving a wedding and a funeral. Unbeknownst to me, I was prophesying my victory in advance through the entire gap season of seven years. It is critically important to always see the function of praise and worship.

Third, to any believer who is afraid of death, let me explain that a believer never loses consciousness in the gap season, the valley of the shadow of death. Death is a shadow. It must bow to the power of God. In earth, we are more

---

[5] "For by him were all things created, that are in Heaven, and that are in earth, visible and invisible, whether they be thrones, or dominions, or principalities, or powers: all things were created by him, and for him." Colossians 1:16 (KJV)

[6] "For God so loved the world, that he gave his only begotten Son, that whosoever believeth in him should not perish, but have everlasting life." John 3:16 (KJV)

[7] "And God blessed them, and God said unto them, Be fruitful, and multiply, and replenish the earth, and subdue it: and have dominion over the fish of the sea, and over the fowl of the air, and over every living thing that moveth upon the earth." Genesis 1:28 (KJV)

WATCH and SEE

aware of our natural reality. In eternity, a believer becomes more and more aware of the eternal realities. For some who believe that a soul sleeps or becomes unaware at death, this is a myth. The Bible tells us, the reality of believers is "We are confident, I say, and willing rather to be absent from the body, and to be present with the Lord." 2 Corinthians 5:8 (KJV)

Lastly, God knows all. He is sovereign. He will use a cataclysmic and unexplainable misfortune (such as, an accident, death, bankruptcy, unemployment, sickness, etc.) as a stage to reveal His awesome power in our gap season. He re-creates us out of our ruins into His marvelous handiworks.

"And I will restore to you the years that the locust hath eaten, the cankerworm, and the caterpillar, and the palmerworm, my great army which I sent among you. And ye shall eat in plenty, and be satisfied, and praise the name of the Lord your God, that hath dealt wondrously with you: and my people shall never be ashamed." Joel 2:25-26 (KJV)

Chapter 3

What time is it?

> *"Therefore we are always confident, knowing that, whilst we are at home in the body, we are absent from the Lord: (For we walk by faith, not by sight:) We are confident, I say, and willing rather to be absent from the body, and to be present with the Lord. Wherefore we labour, that, whether present or absent, we may be accepted of him."*
>
> *II Corinthians 5:6-9 (KJV)*

I remember some of the awesome things that the Lord said, the first time I passed through the tunnel to the other side. He told me to go back and to declare to everyone that Heaven is a real place and that when I get in trouble, I should call upon His name.

But God was going to deal with me again through the process of time, just as He did with Jacob, who saw the angels descending and ascending the ladder that came from Heaven to earth. God was dealing with Jacob to change him from the inside. God was changing Jacob's nature. God dealt with Jacob a second time when he was afraid to meet Esau. Jacob wrestled with the angel all night, and the angel touched the hollow of his thigh; his name was changed. Sometimes, God must deal with us more than once to make us ready to be used of him and to ultimately glorify him.

Well such was the case prior to my second surgery which occurred just seven months after the first. My grandfather, affectionately known by his grandchildren as Popeye, became severely ill while I, ironically, had begun to recuperate from my first surgery. I would spend the day with my grandmother who has now gone on to be with the Lord. We affectionately called her Dear. On this particular day, I took Dear to see Popeye. It was apparent that he was dying. I remember on that day that Dear loved on him as she rubbed his face and just didn't want to leave his hospital bedside. However, when I saw that he was slipping away, fearing for Dear's health because of her serious heart condition, I suggested that we leave.

We left his bedside and by the time that we returned home, my grandfather had died. We planned his funeral. It had become apparent while I was recuperating from the first surgery that a second surgery would be necessary. I remember delaying my second surgery so that I would not miss the funeral. I attended his funeral, and wanted so badly to serve as an active pallbearer, but could not because of the injuries I had sustained from my accident. Popeye's funeral took place and he was buried.

Just a few days later, at the hospital, I went through the second surgery by the grace of God. The purpose of this surgery was to resolve a new problem that had developed during my recovery. On this Saturday, I remember it so well because my wife Ronaé, and my daughter Monaé, had come to the hospital to see me. Monaé was two years old. I enjoyed their visit that Saturday morning, and I was feeling relatively okay. After they left, a group of young people from New York along with, Bishop Roan Faulkner, came to visit me. Because I was the National Youth Choir Director for the United Churches of Jesus Christ, I was glad to see some of the choir members who had traveled so far accompanying Bishop Faulkner on the hospital visit. They brought me an appreciation plaque (as their choir director), prayed with me, greatly encouraged me, and then they left. Following their visit, a dear friend of my wife and me, Pastor Druscilla Spence Carmichael came and uplifted me. She prayed with me, and I felt so encouraged and reinvigorated. I was just so happy that I had had such a beautiful morning filled with inspirational visits.

As I was sitting on the side of the bed, preparing to eat my lunch, which was situated on my bedside table, suddenly, without any warning, a sharp pain began to grip me in my right leg. The pain was so gripping that it instantly weakened me. The weakness was so immediate that it began to overtake my entire system. I knew that something bad was happening to me physically, but I did not understand what this could be.

I thought, let me call the nurse. I attempted to reach for the call button that was wired to my bed, but the very motion of reaching for the button and then pressing it required more energy than I could muster. I didn't have any strength left. I thought, let me pull the phone, which was on my bed, so I could call someone; the phone was too heavy to pull towards me. I couldn't even find the strength to yell for the nurse or the doctor, or attempt to call my wife, parents, or pastor by phone. I needed to call for others, but just didn't have the strength to do so.

The weakness overtook me and captivated my body. Despite this, amazingly I managed to tuck my hands under my legs, to lift them onto the bed, and as my strength gave way, I fell backward onto the mattress. I don't know how I was able to gather my legs. I felt my spirit being drawn out of my body. I had experienced this feeling only once before in the immediate aftermath of the accident. I knew that I was dying, and I couldn't call for help. I couldn't even call my pastor by phone. I tried to reach others, but didn't have the strength. In that moment, I tried to reach God, so I began to sing, *Just in Time*, by the Voices of Supreme (1974).

I remembered the verse.

> *There was a man who had been sick for a long time.*
> *Doctor's had given up and this worried his family's mind.*
> *But this man had suffered and believed with all of his might,*
> *That all God's children have to suffer pain and strife.*

I remembered singing the chorus.

> *Just in time, just in time, just in time.*
> *Jesus came, just in time.*

As I was singing this, the nurse walked by my door. She peeked her head in.

It's so strange that I had not yet relied on God's direction to call for His help when I was in trouble. First, I tried to reach others. But when I sang to God, I believe that He summoned the nurse on my behalf. It's amazing how God allowed her to hear my song, as I was too weak to belt out a melody.

And she asked, "Mr. Johnson, are you okay?"

I shook my head to say, "no." Then she came into the room, and she took my blood pressure.

I remember hearing her scream, "Oh my God, Oh my God!"

She called for the emergency relief using my call button.

I remember hearing so many footsteps rushing into the room. I remember seeing the nurse's horrified expression—it was fear personified. I saw a flurry of medical staff rush into the room, and I felt my spirit completely leaving my body. Again, I went back through the tunnel. I had immediate memory from my first time in the tunnel just months ago at the scene of my accident. But this time, I was moving faster than the speed of light, so it felt. And as I moved through the tunnel, towards the light, my position in the tunnel was different from the first entry. The first time, I was facing Heaven on the other side, and I was going towards the light. This time, I was being pulled into the light while I faced earth, as God was summoning me back to Himself. I was watching and observing as I was pulled into the light backward. When I got to the other side, I began to recognize where I was as the light shone behind me into the tunnel.

I was aware that I remained in the tunnel closest to the other side with my back turned to the light. I began to hear the familiar sound of the River of Life flowing behind me. I had seen the river during my first out of body experience.

I remember how crystal clear and beautiful it was. This time, however, I could not see the river; the memory of its flow was so clear and comforting. This time, the Lord began to speak to me as if He were asking me the question of all ages:

"M A R C U S
W H A T
A R E
Y O U
G O I N G
T O
D O?"

And I knew His voice. I remembered hearing it months earlier. When you hear the voice of God, it is like no other voice you have ever heard.

For me, the voice of God had an authoritatively powerful tone. It was consoling and yet strong. To my ears, His voice sounded majestic and Heavenly. It sounded perfectly loud and quiet, all at once. It was if the very sky were talking. I could hear life all around me, and His voice pierced the moment. I was not afraid. God spoke to me from outside of the tunnel and as He spoke, His voice approached me at the edge of the tunnel. As He continued to speak, I got inside of the sound, and I was engulfed by it. I remember feeling protected from death, as His voice became a part of the light. Although death had pushed me to that point, death was nowhere to be found. Apparently, it had fled. I was centered, safely tucked into the voice of God.

I knew it was God, and He was asking me did I want to live or die. Did I want to enter my Heavenly home now and stay, or did I want to return to my body, on the earth? I knew that is what He meant by asking what I was going to do.

Then as I looked towards earth, my vision was intense and telescopic, looking down at what appeared to be eons and eons of time in the tunnel. Positioned at the very threshold of eternity and time, I could experience the divide between the spiritual and the physical the terrestrial and the celestial realms. I knew, at this point, that I could cross over and never return to earth again and enjoy *the hope of glory*.

The scripture that Paul spoke began to reverberate in my spirit, "...and willing rather to be absent from the body, and to be present with the Lord." 2 Corinthians 5:8 (KJV) I knew that it was true.

I began to hear Paul say, "For I am in a strait betwixt two, having a desire to depart, and to be with Christ; which is far better: Nevertheless, to abide in the flesh is more needful for you." Philippians 1:23-24 (KJV)

Thus, if I go on and be with the Lord, it would be far better. I can escape the pain, the misery, and the challenges. To remain is to finish the work that God had given to me: to be a blessing to those that He had designated me to serve in ministry.

I was trying to decide, and it was so amazing, as I looked down through the tunnel back to earth, where I had come. I saw my wife and my daughter standing together. They were holding hands at the end of the tunnel. I remember that they looked expressionless. It was a very solemn look. I knew that their faces embodied the sadness that they would experience if I died. They would both know the reality of sadness if my wife lost her husband and my daughter lost her father. As I looked closer, I saw that they were in God's hands. I knew that they would cope, but I could not dismiss the fact that they would be greatly impacted by my death.

Then as I began to observe even closer, still, I saw something I had not seen at first. There was something growing behind them. It was a huge ministry. I noticed that the ministry became bigger than my wife and my daughter. As it grew, they began to shrink inside of it—for they, too, were a part of the ministry. The entire ministry was growing out of God's hands.

I feel the need to be clear, at this point, that huge ministry was not synonymous with a large building, money, and flashing lights. I didn't see cameras, and cash and cars. I didn't see mansions and television screens and red carpets. I saw a spiritual image of divine work as though God freeze framed my purpose with unparalleled clarity in high definition such that I knew with the mind of the Spirit it was my ministry.

I cannot recall the details of it. The ministry was mammoth in size proportional to the image of my wife and daughter who were in God's hands. The ministry was unfinished, and my name was written across the image. There was no way for me to escape the reality of this imagery.

God was saying to me that if I left the tunnel, stepped into the light, and crossed over, I would leave incomplete work in the earth—my purpose and my destiny, my ministry would remain unfulfilled. I knew what God wanted me to do. I knew God wanted me to go back to earth. That's why He allowed me to remain in the tunnel transfixed, facing the earth where the ministry was. The ministry was not in Heaven. The ministry was not in glory. The ministry was in the earth, and only I could come back and complete my portion of the ministry that God had given to me.

Because I loved God, the same love that compelled me to want a testimony at the age of twelve became the same love for God that caused me to want to please him and go back and finish the work that He had assigned to me. God had linked my prayer at the age of twelve to this point in eternity.

My dear reader, I can hear the question you are asking. And the answer is a resounding "Yes". Our prayers reach from time into eternity and turn things around.

I remember saying to God, "I'll go back and finish the work."

I could feel the reality of God's delight with my choice as His light radiated on my back.

I never saw God as I never saw him the first time. But his presence was so overwhelming, compelling, consuming, and undeniable. He filled the entire space. My intimate awareness of Him allowed my spirit to know him in a way that was so affirming!

I remember saying, "God, if I'm going to go back, please give me the strength to fight."

In that moment, I was aware that death was now present. Death can travel through the tunnel, but as it approaches the light death weakens and loses the ability to push and thrust a believer to Heaven. However, I knew that I would have to fight death to re-enter time and return to the earth. I knew this because of the revelation of truth that was so pervasive in the tunnel. Death could not stop me from doing the work of God in the earth, but death was glad for me to be gone; at least my impact in my physical body in the earth would be incomplete. Trying to thwart my impact in the earth, death was going to try to stop me from coming back and re-entering my body.

But God gave me strength to believe. I remember being imbued with God's strength. This felt like divine energy was infused into my spirit as I begin to press, to fight my way back through death in the tunnel. The scripture in Paul's words came to my mind, "I press toward the mark for the prize of the high calling of God in Christ Jesus." Philippians 3:14 (KJV)

I had never seen the scripture this way before. I always thought that I would press to go towards God, towards Heaven, and towards eternity. But upon this encounter, I understood that sometimes we must press through the struggle of death to be able to get to our earthly assignment. The completion of an assignment becomes the prize of the high calling, not just in Heaven, but even in the earth. There is glory invested in the earth, for us to experience on this side.

Still, God gave me strength, and I fought my way back, through death in the tunnel. Death tried to block me as I fought. "...because greater is he that is in you, than he that is in the world." 1 John 4:4b (KJV) With the strength of God, I fought my way back, defeating death in the tunnel. Death fell backward, overpowered by the strength of God; I was released through my faith and determination to please God.

Instead of my spirit re-entering my body, my spirit (the real me) was in the ceiling of the hospital room. I literally hovered over my body as an onlooker. I began to watch the medical team work on my lifeless body below. The details of their medical procedures were astounding as I observed the nurses and doctors that crowded into the room. I watched as more medical staff pressed through the cramped doorway. Two doctors climbed onto the bed to beat on my chest, simultaneously, to resuscitate me. Amazingly as they began to come into the room, I watched a nurse run out of the room. There I saw my lifeless body lying on the bed. I saw them ripping off my clothing and injecting me multiple times in my abdomen. I observed every detail.

And then, as my spirit was in the ceiling of the hospital room with God, He said to me, "Watch and See. Watch and See."

As I continued to observe, I could see more details of the chaotic scene. I saw the resuscitation machine arrive, and it hit the nurse on her shin. I literally heard her say, "ouch," and I watched her grimace in pain. Almost mechanically, the nurse steadied her focus and resolve and returned to the resuscitation effort. I watched medical staff scrambling in the room. I saw many of the attendants, who had responded to the hospital resuscitation code announced overhead, stand motionless. The attendants had a painful expression as though seeing the death of a young man was traumatic. Maybe for some of the motionless young doctors in the room, this was their first encounter with death, losing a patient who was just too young to die at twenty-six years old. I sensed that they felt helpless.

Finally, I watched a doctor place paddles on my bare chest and administer a shock. My body lurched upward from the bed, but there was no response.

And he repeated it again. My body leaped again and there was no response.

After the second defibrillation attempt, the two doctors climbed back on the bed and continued to pound my chest. It was like I was watching a dance in the middle of mayhem, but there was no music. As the room began to fall silent, the head doctor asked the nurse, "What time is it?"

She replied. I remembered seeing the head doctor frown, and he pumped his fist yelling, "he's gone." It was as though the frenetic freight train that had careened through the room in all attempts to resuscitate me, in one moment halted.

One of the doctors beating on my chest climbed off the bed as though he realized nothing else could be done. Maybe he was listening to the head doctor, or maybe he instinctively felt, after no response from my heart that his attempts were futile. He seemed to realize that it was over.

The other doctor remained motionless, as though he were in a trance. He just wouldn't stop pounding on my chest. I watched as the head doctor stamped his foot upon the floor, and struck the leg of the lone doctor who kept pounding my chest. He yelled very loudly this time, "I said he's gone."

It was as if the exasperation with the continued resuscitation attempts had made him angry. I knew that he couldn't understand why the lone doctor would continue attempts to revive me after his commanding announcement that I had died. I was gone. Surely, as the senior physician in the room, he had seen patients die, so he knew the point at which there was nothing else that they could do to get me back.

Subsequently, the head doctor put his hands in his pocket and spun away from the staff to gaze out of the window into the day's Saturday afternoon sky. It was like that one lone doctor was operating on auto-pilot. God had arrested him. I was clear that he was acting outside of his own volition and power. In that moment, his will was to fulfill the momentary purpose that God had designed and that was to remain in contact with my heart, strike by strike, rhythmically simulating my pulse until my heartbeat returned. God had called him for such a time as this. Hence, he continued beating on my chest.

It is nonsensical to think that even though God will do a miracle, He will use a human being to participate. God will allow frail people to take part in a great work. In the face of the possibility of insubordination, the lone doctor ignored the command of his superior and kept beating on my chest. Although unaware, he was subordinate only to the Great Physician. With strike after strike of his fist, his motion was not predicated on the response from my body, as he was using his own momentum waiting to feel my heart resume beating.

Then God said to me in the ceiling again, "Watch and See. Watch and See." He wanted me to watch the physical impossibility; to watch how the doctors and nurses were responding; to take in the utter doom and gloom that was in the room; to watch the majority that had given up; to watch the lifeless body on the bed—a corpse, a hollow shell. But then, He wanted me to see the one doctor who I believe represented Jesus Christ, the Chief Physician, who would not give up on us.

"If a man die, shall he live again? all the days of my appointed time will I wait, till my change come." Job 14:14 (KJV)

I'm not giving up on you.

As the lone doctor continued to beat on my chest, the Lord finally said to me once more, "Watch and See." The nurses dropped their heads. I saw one nurse grab my hand, and she cried saying, "Mr. Johnson don't die like this. You can't go like this. You can't do this."

And then, seamlessly, I felt the Lord lowering my spirit out of the ceiling. He began to slip my spirit back into my body, like a hand in a glove, with great mastery and precision. As He did this, I could hear the faint sound of the lone doctor pounding on my chest. I couldn't feel his violent pounding at first. It was as though there was a momentary lag between my spirit's bodily reentry and my physically regaining feeling. As I kept listening, I could hear the pounding, and it grew louder, and louder, and then I could feel the discomfort. And then pain… I remember having the awareness in my mind that God was bringing my body back to life, and I felt joy. I was in the body, but I didn't yet have the strength to open my mouth and respond. The pounding got louder and louder as it began to synchronize with the growing pain that I began to feel as the lone doctor struck my chest. As I felt more pain, I was getting stronger. With each wave of pain came a surge of strength. The pain was signaling my strength so that I could respond.

I finally got up enough strength all at once and I said, "ouch."

WATCH and SEE

I opened my eyes and I saw that everyone collectively was shocked.

I instantaneously remembered that saying ouch was not appropriate. I had to give God the glory in this room, in my body, in the presence of the medical team. God had performed a miracle.

I repeated over and over again, "Thank you, Jesus." "Thank you, Jesus." "Thank you, Jesus."

The doctors and the nurses were utterly astounded. The head doctor whipped his body around turning towards me and away from the window. He gazed at me suddenly, realizing that I was back.

Next the doctor who was pounding on my chest began to gaze into my eyes. I could tell that he was shocked. Clearly, I had scared incredible life into him.

He leaped off my chest as the entire emotion of the room changed from sadness to a flurry of activities to reinstate stability into my physical body. I could feel various injections as the medical team began administering many different medications all at once. It was as though someone was performing a task on almost every square inch of my body. I could also feel that the entire room was reeling from the awareness that I had died but was now revived.

God was doing so much in this moment. It is very important to understand that the most magnificent power of God is resurrection power: literally, from death to life.

From my hospital bed, I had a view into the hallway. At this point, my family had begun to arrive, and I remember specifically the moment when Lady Alberta (Mother Saunders) and my parents, Mr. Mottomoes and Mrs. Elouise Johnson stood in my room. I also remember seeing my wife.

The miraculous testimony of God's power began to unfold as He not only had delivered me from a pulmonary embolism (blood clot in my lungs), but also, He had given my wife supernatural willingness to return to the hospital. Even though my wife and Monaé had visited me earlier that day and left to go to the mall, suddenly while in the mall, the Lord spoke to my wife as if summoning her back to the hospital.

Remember, in 1983, there were no cell phones. Social media and email didn't exist. I couldn't tweet or send an instant message to my wife or anyone for that matter. I couldn't change my Facebook status to explain what had just transpired. But thank God, my wife remained plugged into God. Because Ronaé had been contacted by the Holy Ghost, her Lord, back she came to the hospital. When she arrived the Presiding Bishop's son, Jason, met her in the lobby and explained that the hospital was trying to reach her by phone at home. Understanding that she was needed upstairs, because I had just been resuscitated, she raced up to my room. As she arrived, I was being prepped to go down for emergency X-rays.

As Ronaé and Mother Saunders drew closer to me, Mother Saunders said, "We must pray."

I gazed into Ronaé's eyes, and I saw the pain and terror in her face as she began to cry. I knew that she could not reconcile how she had just left me in good spirits and improving health only to return to such a catastrophic situation. I read the words, "What happened?" in her eyes. And as she cried, I began to cry. Mother Saunders intervened, "Oh no, no, no. These must be tears of joy because God is going to do a mighty work in this. And He's wiping away these tears from our eyes."

We began to pray before I was rolled out of the room. I saw some of my family and church family members in the hallway. I waved my hand in the air to signal to them that I would be fine and into the elevator I went.

"To every thing there is a season, and a time to every purpose under the heaven...I know that, whatsoever God doeth, it shall be for ever: nothing can be put to it, nor any thing taken from it: and God doeth it, that men should fear before him." Ecclesiastes 3:1,14 (KJV) God uses the process of time to accomplish His eternal purposes.

Words of Wisdom to Readers

It is important to obtain a Godly perspective to see the unseen. Through faith, we can focus on our purpose and the status of our assignments in the earth. Sometimes we must decide—will I stop or will I finish the course of my life (my purpose or given assignment). Did you know that we can leave without finishing our assignments? Let's consider Paul's testimony. For Paul said, "I have fought a good fight, I have finished my course, I have kept the faith:" II Timothy 4:7 (KJV)

Although we can prematurely leave earth with unfinished assignments, it's in the focus with the eyes of God, that we can determine if the course is finished or whether we must continue. Knowing the heart of God, we must press on to complete our assignments. If we choose, He will give us the grace to finish them. Therefore, our focus should be to hold onto the promise keeper while we wait to apprehend the promise.

Chapter 4

A RAINBOW IN THE FALLS

> *"But my God shall supply all your need according to his riches in glory by Christ Jesus."* Philippians 4:19 (KJV)

When I was in a hospital based in Baltimore (Hospital A), I stayed there for quite some time—several weeks. We were approaching Thanksgiving Day of that year. I was not getting better. Although I could bear my own weight minimally, being able to move and to walk was virtually impossible. My orthopedic surgeon felt he was at his wits end with my case. He no longer knew what else to do for me. He had been treating me for several years now and with all the surgeries that I had received, seven at this point, he felt that he was reaching his end. My condition was very complicated. I honestly believe that he was doing his best to help me. He learned of an orthopedic medicine specialist in Buffalo, New York, and asked me if I would be willing to travel there to be examined. I consented and arrangements were made for me to fly to Buffalo to see the specialist.

It was Thanksgiving Eve; my wife, daughter, and me rode from Hospital A to the then Baltimore Washington International (BWI) airport. At the ticket counter, we were assisted by airline attendants who put me in a wheelchair. The attendants then took me to the gate where I was transferred into an airplane wheelchair which was engineered to navigate through the narrow aisles of the airplane. When we arrived at my seat, the airline stewards physically lifted me out of the special wheelchair and placed me in my aisle seat.

As we proceeded on that flight getting comfortable was very difficult. For several weeks prior, I was hospitalized and bedridden because I could barely stand. Therefore, with the various maneuvers that it took to get me from the hospital to the airport, to the ticket counter, to the gate and finally to my seat, my body was physically exhausted. I anticipated each maneuver before it happened, and I could not rest as I knew that our trip was just beginning. Up to this point, my pain medication had been routinely administered via IV drip. But this trip meant that I would only be able to take my medication orally as my wife administered it. Not only was I in tremendous physical pain, but I knew that with each pill it would take longer for the medication to take effect. I was very anxious because I had left the familiarity of the hospital, the regular medical team, and the regularity of my routine. I was meeting a new specialist out of state knowing that my doctor of almost six years was exasperated with my case. Consequently, I relied on my wife to talk and pray me through what seemed like an extremely long plane ride as we trusted God to keep us safe. Put simply, we just prayed that God would keep our many pieces together.

This was my wife's first time flying. I had flown many times before in previous decades since my youth. And yet this day, my wife was challenged as a first-time flyer, with a very sick husband, a young child in tow and an unknown journey ahead.

When we arrived at the airport in Buffalo, the airline stewards lifted me off the plane. At the gate, we readied ourselves to go to the baggage claim and call the hotel to send a shuttle to pick us up. Shockingly, the airline staff demanded that we return their wheelchair at the gate. At approximately 260 lbs, there was no way that my wife could transport me. With that sudden turn of events, we were instantly left stranded.

Up to this point, we had never thought about it. It had never occurred to us that because I was wheelchair bound, that I would only be able to be transported by wheelchair upon arrival in Buffalo. No one had suggested to us that the airline would lend us a wheelchair in the airport but not beyond.

Emphatically, we said to the airline staff that we couldn't manage without it.

And they responded, "this is our property. You cannot take the wheelchair."

Now you may be thinking, "how could you not know that you would need a loaner wheelchair?" I would remind you that I had grown accustomed to practically living in hospitals where wheelchairs, crutches, walkers, and other assistive devices are abundant and easily given. I did not own a wheelchair because I had been living in the hospital for quite some time.

With determination, my wife began to use the hotel phone lists and call each hotel to find out if there were any that had wheelchairs. We discovered at that time that the accessibility for physically challenged persons, as we know it today, did not yet exist. And in the mid to late-1980s, most of the hotels were not yet handicapped accessible with ramps, wider doorways, and available wheelchairs.

After several moments of intense discussion, the airline gate attendants relented, and we were allowed to take the wheelchair down to baggage claim only. We were told, "this chair cannot leave the airport." Just like that, with no sympathy and no feeling, it was our only option.

WATCH and SEE

And I could feel the tears swelling in my eyes.

There were so many great challenges, and we were trying so hard just to live successfully in such a crazy situation. It was Thanksgiving Eve and what did we have to be thankful for?

We were so greatly challenged until we began to pray. Yes, right there in the airport, we prayed. We felt desperate. We were in Buffalo, New York and were unable to get from there to the hotel to the doctor's office because we didn't have a wheelchair.

My wife assured me that she would get us help. In a flurry, she raced over to a bank of pay phones, asking passersby, travelers, and airport personnel if there was just a single wheelchair available anywhere that we could rent.

Moreover, God had promised to supply all our needs. Considering all the phone calls that she made, one hotel, just one recommended a limousine service. This was certainly our plan B, but we soon discovered that it was our only plan if we were going to get out of the airport to the hotel and to the doctor's office on time.

We contacted the limousine service, and the owner answered the phone. He willingly accepted our story and quickly agreed to assist us. Thinking that he would send a driver, to our surprise, he came to our rescue as the driver. He physically picked me up and carried me to the limousine. I was very heavy and Tony, a little Italian limousine driver, could not have weighed more than 160 lbs. But he lifted me, placed me inside of the limousine and took us to the Marriott hotel in Buffalo. They were the only hotel that we could find that was wheelchair accessible. When we arrived at the hotel, the Marriott provided us with a wheelchair; our driver Tony wheeled me into the lobby where the strangest thing occurred.

Immediately, the Marriott front desk staff looked at me and began making arrangements for our room. My wife and I noticed that the staff kept going into the back office and coming out again smiling. We proceeded to complete the reservation paperwork and then they escorted us to our hotel room.

But we were shocked because we had requested one modest room for two adults and one child. However, we were escorted to a lavish suite.

I immediately said to the attendant, "we didn't order a suite," as I began to compute mentally how exorbitantly priced this suite must be.

The attendant replied, "we know."

My wife and I said, "we can't pay for a suite," knowing that this medical trip would be reimbursed by my worker's compensation benefits. We were thinking, we can't afford this. We had reserved simple accommodations because we were forced to live on a meager budget.

The attendant said, "Don't worry. This is your accommodation during your stay with us."

We entered the suite, and it was gorgeous. Not only was it handicap accessible, but there were so many areas. There was a living area with multiple sofas, a dining area, hallway bath, a master bedroom with full bath and an office. There were wooden and carpeted floors with wall to wall draperies, marble countertops and beautiful wallpaper. The furniture was luxurious and plush with deeply cushioned seats. There were ornate lamps and lights in the ceiling. The room was on a very high floor and as we looked out of the picturesque windows, we could see snowcapped rooftops and mountains in the distance. The view was stunning. All we could think is how did we get here, and when were the police coming to escort us out?

Later that day, Tony, the limousine driver took us to Lewiston, New York which is situated near the Canadian border, Lake Ontario, and Niagara Falls. There we went to see the orthopedic medicine specialist. He conducted his practice in his home, and Tony carried me through his garage. He then lifted me onto the examination table once inside the specialist's office. Tony delivered my wife and daughter safely inside, also, then he waited in the vicinity for us to finish.

We were in a very modest square house with square rooms that were quite small. Looking at his home you never would have considered that he was in such high demand worldwide and he was an accomplished medical author. Amazingly, he had agreed to examine me. My wife and I had placed our hopes in so many doctors up to this point, that we cautiously considered the bleak possibility that this trip could somehow hold a new answer to my declining condition.

He conducted his examination as he manipulated my legs and examined the network of surgical scars that mapped my back like railroad tracks.

He looked at me and said, "I will help you."

It was such a relief to hear him say these promising words. I suddenly felt as if I hadn't breathed in months before now. He could help me. The outlook on my case seemed finally as if there was hope coming. There was a sunrise in the distance. There was a possibility that this episodic hell was ending. The page was turning and my recovery was coming.

"But my God will supply all your need, according to His riches in glory." God takes our entire earth experience and in His hands, He molds every need into a singular need. Throughout our years, He dispenses resources to cover the sum of our need in life.

As he continued his examination he would say, "You're hurting here. You have pain in your neck over here. You are hurting here in your back."

And we wondered, how could he know all of this. He explained that from his experience he could determine the damage that was done in my spine. On his examination table he began the process of feeling the back of my spine to find the coccyx (the tail bone). He then prepared an injection with the longest needle

WATCH and SEE

I had ever seen. When I saw it, I was terrified to know that he was preparing to insert that needle into my spine.

The cylindrical tube that held the milky white injection was about eight inches long and quite wide connecting to the scariest needle I had ever seen in my life. I had become a veteran in the hospital, at this point, taking pills and getting injections daily. I had stood by my wife's bedside prior to the birth of my daughter and saw the needle as the anesthesiologist administered her epidural. By comparison, I had never seen anything like this. This needle looked like a submarine attached to a torpedo, and he was preparing to fire a missile into my spine.

Although I took great comfort in his promise to help me, I couldn't relax anticipating this needle.

He said to me, "Lay on your stomach and hold onto the steel bar overhead at the top of the table. Squeeze it as hard as you can, and let me insert the needle but do not move. This could permanently damage you if the needle hits the wrong nerve."

So, I lay on my stomach, and I began to reflect over all that we had gone through up to this point, with all the incidents and all the circumstances, with all the unforeseen barriers, God had always provided for us.

"But my God shall supply all of your need...."

I held onto that bar, and I squeezed it with all I knew as he inserted the injection into the base of my coccyx bone. To say that it was painful is inadequate. The pain was an excruciating, torturous pain. But I wanted help. I needed something that was going to prevent complete paralysis. I needed something that would enable me to function and that would minimize the horrific chronic pain.

I don't remember exactly how long it took for him to put the injection in. But it took a while because the needle tip was unusually large, and all the medication from the huge vial had to be emptied into my spine. And then I had to tell him where I could feel the sensation of medication and where I could feel his hands on my spine.

In the hospital, whenever I received a large spinal injection, I first received local anesthesia at the injection site. But this was different because I had to direct him by the sensations that I felt in my spine. So, numbing me with local anesthesia was not an option. I grabbed the bar overhead, and I squeezed it, and I bore the pain until he was done.

This injection was filled with a steroid. The plan was that he would realign my spine. He would literally manipulate my back and use the steroid to decrease the inflammation that was contributing to my chronic pain. His goal was to retrain my spine causing it to realign over time and hopefully this would thwart any impending surgery. It was a mix of a chiropractic manipulation and a rehabilitative training exercise with medication. As long as my spine was misaligned, the imbalance would pinch nerves that would cause chronic pain and spasms.

We went through the ordeal and after he completed the injection, I laid on my belly, motionless. This immobilization allowed the medication to flow up my spinal cord, and it re-stabilized my spine. He began to explain that he would need to see me monthly to try to get a positive result from this radical treatment.

As I lay there, a daunting thought occurred to me. As heavy as I was, and as difficult as it was for Tony to lift me and carry me, how was I going to get back to the hotel? Would he drop me? And once we got to the hotel, and I was wheeled back to my room, it would just be my wife, daughter, and me. Would my wife be able to manage all of this?

But God would give her the strength. God would give her the ability.

As Tony came into the office, he picked me up and placed me back in the limousine. It was obvious that he felt badly for us. This was the Thanksgiving holiday. It was cold, and there was snow on the ground. But he decided to drive us on an impromptu excursion. He took us to see the Niagara Falls. It was such a scenic view as we peered out at all the sites.

He stopped and let my wife and daughter exit as they stood at the edge of the falls. Through the window, I watched the water spray on their faces as their hair blew in the wind. I saw the great expanse of the canyon filled with water. There was so much noise as the violent currents flowed everywhere at the same time. At their backs, I could see a rainbow in the falls amid the mist of the rapidly flowing water. It was undisturbed, multidimensional, and so colorful. I sat in the back of that limo and I wished that I could grab the rainbow that appeared to sit on top of the water. I quietly knew in my heart that God had not forgotten us. He had allowed Tony, a stranger to become such a kind friend. Tony created such a positive and needed distraction amidst a tumultuous day. In that moment, I was thankful on Thanksgiving Eve. For God, had given me so many promises and that was apparent with each colorful band of the rainbow in view. I was thankful, not for my plight, not for my pain, but for this warm moment that seemed carved out of such a cold and rocky day.

We returned to the hotel after about an hour's ride back from the Falls.

When we arrived, Tony obtained the wheelchair, placed me in it and wheeled me up to the room. At the room's doorstep, he physically lifted me up out of the chair and placed me onto the bed. It was from that point on that my wife, with my cooperation, had to lift me from the bed into the wheelchair when I needed to use the handicapped bathroom or dine at the table in our hotel room.

There were still many more surprises awaiting us. Upon our return to the room, there was a fruit basket placed for us on the long wooden dining room table. It was a thank you for choosing this hotel for our stay in Buffalo, and to let us know that the staff was more than willing to accommodate us.

WATCH and SEE

My wife and I were baffled. This just didn't make any sense.

God kept balancing us out by sending pleasantries right before or after turmoil. He was the master architect. He was the overseer. No matter how bad circumstances looked or felt, He would send a blessing. Even when we tried to get into a slump of depression, He would engineer a gift for us. I want to suggest to you that there is a place of praise to God where we should give thanks in the face of impossibilities. On this Thanksgiving Eve, we understood that in everything we should give thanks. My family would be thankful. On this trip, God had supplied all our needs.

"In every thing give thanks: for this is the will of God in Christ Jesus concerning you." 1 Thessalonians 5:18 (KJV)

Given the circumstances, our only option for meals was to use room service, so we stayed in the hotel one more day to allow my body to recuperate from the treatment. On the following morning, we were ready to check-out.

My wife helped me into the wheelchair, and I rolled myself down to the front desk to check-out. While there, I said to the attendant, "We were promised a regular nightly rate because we did not request the Executive Suite that we were given." As you can imagine, my stomach flip flopped as I knew that this moment would inevitably come. Somehow, I was not sure that they would honor their commitment to us.

The front desk attendant said, "Don't worry. The hotel fee will be the same as a regular double occupancy room."

After all this mysteriousness and secrecy, I asked, "why all of this special treatment?"

She replied, "you know why."

I responded, "no I don't."

And she said, "yes you do."

I firmly said, "I do not know."

She asked, "what is your name?"

I said, "Marcus Johnson."

She said, "we know who you are. We know you are really Luther Vandross and we know you are traveling incognito. Would you sing us a song?"

I said, "Miss, I am not Luther Vandross."

I must confess at that time in my life, I was perhaps the only person in the universe that had no clue who Luther Vandross was. I mean, I had heard his name, but I wasn't familiar with any of his famous hits. I was so bewildered.

She continued to insist that I was Luther traveling incognito.

And so, sitting at the front desk in my wheelchair, I said repeatedly to her, "I am not Luther Vandross."

She replied, "Alright. It's obvious you don't want anyone to know who you are, but we all recognize you. We contacted our owner who authorized us to give you the best accommodations and hospitality during your stay with us."

I looked at her and then I looked at my wife.

I said, "you really believe that I am Luther Vandross?" So, I took out my driver's license, and I presented to her.

She looked like she halfway believed me and halfway did not.

She said, "Mr. Johnson this has been a mistake on our part, but because it is our error, we cannot and will not charge you. You look like Luther, the famous singer and you are welcome to come back to this hotel at any time. Your fee will be the same as if you rented a regular room for two."

As she smiled, I thought to myself ironically, "But my God will supply all of my need according to his riches in glory." Our God is rich, and He takes pleasure in lavishing his children with blessings.

Next, Tony returned on that last day, lifted me and put me back into the limousine. He drove us to the airport as we recounted our experience at the hotel.

It became an opportunity for my wife and I to share with him the gospel of Jesus Christ and to discuss the things of God. He began to pour his heart out to us. Not only was God supplying all our need, but the limousine driver's need as well. For Tony was providing a service for us and in that process, he became available for God to bless him too.

The question could be posed, what was the purpose of this trip? Was it for me to begin receiving treatments from the specialist or was it for Tony to hear the gospel of Jesus Christ? Or was it an opportunity for me to recount to you what God allowed me to learn? I submit that there were many purposes that God had intended and that those purposes are still being accomplished today as you read this chapter.

Tony asked us to pray for him, and this began a relationship for the next eighteen months, as I would travel back and forth to Buffalo, New York. Tony would provide the transportation as he would pick me up at the airport and take me to the Marriott hotel. Over the course of this time, many family and friends took turns accompanying me to Buffalo so that my wife could go to work. Because I could not make the trip alone, my travel companions included my parents, my grandmother Dear, my brothers Ministers Stevie and David, my sister Co-Pastor Chelly, my soon to be brother-in-law Bishop Peter Edmund, Sr., and his brother Bishop Dexter Edmund, Sr.

Tony would take us to Lewiston to the specialist for my treatments. During these months, Tony talked about his life and what he needed while I, along with my companions, ministered to him. We continued to share the testimony of what God had done in my life up to that point.

WATCH and SEE

I expressed the "Watch and See" encounter with God at the scene of my accident and again at the hospital with the pulmonary embolism. God began this process with all the persons in my path. The Marriott became a home away from home while in Buffalo. I watched God operate in a very unconventional way as He supplied the spiritual need of so many persons along this journey according to his riches in glory.

As time passed, I would be able to do more than I thought. For no matter what fallen state I found myself, there was always a rainbow (God's promised covenant) in that fall, as a reminder that God had made so many promises to me and to my family, and that He would keep his word.

Words of Wisdom to Readers

Sometimes we ask the Lord, "what will you have me to do?" But He has already set everything up for us such that everyone in the journey will take part in what He has foreordained. On these trips, we stayed at the same Marriott each time where we could minister to their staff. We met Tony each time as he transported us during our stay, and we ministered to him. We continued to see the specialist and ministered to him as well. Throughout the entire experience, we continued to trust in God as He ministered to us.

So, wherever God has allowed you to pass through or to be stationed, look for your audience. Who has He placed in your path? Know that they are there by default as your ministry targets. In school, at work, in your neighborhood, in the market, at chemotherapy, in the courtroom, these persons are your ministry assignments. We ask the Lord, "what will you have me to do?" But the answer on a base level is not that deep or complex. Now, some circumstances will pose this question, and God will provide specificity and clarity. But on a simpler level, choose to accept your assignment to do all that He has already placed in your path to do. God has made a covenant with you, He will not only supply your need and the needs of others along your path, but also, He will reward you for accomplishing your assignments. What are you waiting for? Your ministry assignments are already waiting on you. And God's favor is ensured by the presence of the rainbow.

Bonus Words of Wisdom to Readers

God was gracious to allow me to discover my divine assignments for this season of my life. I desired to work for God after He healed me. In my limited perspective, I thought only after I was healed, I could have a greater impact in God's kingdom. I was overlooking my current God given assignments in comparison to what I saw others doing. Yet, my assignment lay in my lap. God put it there. Please understand the principle here, God will only pay and reward you for doing your assignment, not another's. So, to work from sun up to sun down laboriously is a waste of time if at the end of the day, my work, my God given assignments are incomplete. Lord teach us how to number our days and how to do what you have for each of our hands to do. This means I must not pursue a high title or a position unless this is truly what God has assigned to me and not another. Moses was assigned his work and Aaron was assigned his tasks. Paul was assigned his work, Esther was assigned her tasks, while James and John were assigned theirs. John the Baptist was assigned his work, Lydia was assigned her work, Mary was assigned her tasks, and Jesus was assigned his own. In this season, I was assigned my own work as a man in a wheelchair with chronic pain who could barely walk—that was my role.

Clearly understanding and accepting our assignments prevents misalignment, confusion, and delays. Sometimes the assignment is literally to be worked upon. His desire is for me to be taught rather than just to teach others. His desire is for me to be preached to rather than to just preach to others. His desire is for me to be pastored (fathered) rather than to just pastor (shepherd) others. So, whatever His design is for a specific season in life, that must be my work. That is the assignment that I should accept. And at the appointed time, the student becomes the teacher, the parishioner becomes the pastor, the healed becomes the witness for the Great Physician.

Let each abide in his own calling, lest he put his hand to the plow and turn desiring something greater in his own eyes. Work your work while it is day, for God has already promised that He will pay. He will reward us only for completing our assignments. But the path to the reward begins by doing your assigned work (whatever it is) in your assigned season.

Finally, during every challenge and obstacle that halts the fulfillment of our assignment, there is a rainbow. For God has made a covenant with us that He will provide everything we need for the completion of our assignments. And "...he is a rewarder of them that diligently seek him." Hebrews 11:6 (KJV)

Chapter 5

THE ENEMY IN ME (CODEPENDENCY)

"While he was yet speaking, there came also another, and said....And, behold, there came a great wind from the wilderness, and smote the four corners of the house, and it fell....Then Job arose, and rent his mantle, and shaved his head, and fell down upon the ground, and worshipped."
Job 1:16-18,20 (KJV)

And the Lord used my circumstances to demonstrate that I can depend upon no one like Him. What do you do when your problems create more problems?

For me, my problem was chronic back pain. The damage that my body had sustained from nine back surgeries, following my accident, had created a perpetual nightmare. I had stopped walking. I could barely move my legs that were increasingly becoming more and more numb by the day. My pain was so intense that my blood pressure would rise. But because I couldn't walk, other conditions resulted due to my paralysis. The problems were cyclical and intense.

This time, I spent several weeks in Hospital A, and the more they did for me, the more my condition worsened. Since the medical staff had exhausted all potential treatments for my condition, I was subsequently transferred by ambulance to a hospital in Baltimore. There I was told after just a few hours of medical assessment that I should go home—for there was nothing more they could do for me. Seeing my dire condition at home, my primary care physician, who was also a family friend, the late Dr. Elijah Saunders, along with our family pastor, Bishop Monroe Saunders, Sr., refused to let me stay at home and suffer miserably. I was transferred ultimately to another local hospital (Hospital B) where I stayed for more than a month.

There the previous medical assessments were repeated from X-rays, to CAT scans, to psychiatric evaluations to orthopedic and neurological tests. The team was searching for a root cause of my chronic pain beyond the obvious. They knew that I needed medication to minimize my pain. This was done to ultimately attempt to cap my blood pressure, though it remained in a very dangerous high range. However, the aggressive pain medication regimen was affecting my vital body organs as it suppressed my heart rate; I was dying.

In the height of my pain, spasms would rotate from my lower spine into my pelvis. And from my pelvis into my lower spine until the only adequate treatment they could give me was the injection of Morphine and Valium. They would administer it every three hours. It didn't last for three hours, but they couldn't repeat it until the span of three hours had passed to avoid an overdose.

On this particular day, there was a male nurse that was assigned to me. He was my primary nurse for the day. He informed me that he was working a double shift and had asked to be assigned to me.

He stated, "I've worked with you before and I enjoy working with you. So, I will be assigned to your case."

We got along very well and I had no issue with him up to this point.

During that morning I struggled to get pain relief. I informed my male nurse and he said, "I will give you your medication." And he did. He said, "now lay comfortably, and you will start feeling a little better." For about thirty to forty minutes, I did begin to feel a little better, but a little better is relative because I was in so much pain.

After about forty minutes the medication became ineffective—it was wearing off. I knew I had to endure two and a quarter hours before the medication could be re-administered. To someone who is immobile, that's literally 135 minutes—that's 8,100 seconds of waiting. I want to pause here. There is a sensitivity that I still feel for persons who suffer with pain. And to anyone who is challenged to endure what feels like days to your next dose of partial pain relief, I have been where you are. Rest assured, dear friend, God sees. God knows. He has not forsaken you.

I tried not to look at my watch. I tried not to be aware of the time. I tried to find ways of diverting my thoughts. I tried to pray, but it was so hard to be focused when there was so much pain to endure.

But I made my way through; and as I began to approach the next time the medicine could be administered, I pushed my call button. I asked for the nurse, but he didn't show up. After about five minutes, I called for him again. And five minutes became fifteen minutes which became thirty minutes. Thirty minutes became an hour. I should add at this point that my lower extremities were beginning to really weaken. I was losing the ability to use my legs. They were becoming very numb and rubbery, so I couldn't get up and walk. I had a steel trapeze attached to my bed. It had hooks that I could reach up and grab onto like a pulley. This allowed me to pull my body weight and shift myself in the bed. Because I couldn't use my feet or body anymore for leverage, I would try to ease the pressure of my body weight by changing positions. These minor readjustments would bring momentary relief.

But nothing was working and the nurse wouldn't come. When I would call the nurse at the reception desk I was told, "I've called your nurse, he should be there by now." But he did not come.

Finally, three hours later, he showed up.

I was drenched with sweat from hours of chronic pain.

I demanded, "what happened? I've been waiting for you. I'm hurting so bad."

And he said, "I did come."

"No, you didn't. You gave me the first dosage, but those three hours passed, and I needed another dose. You never came. It's been six hours since my last injection."

"Yes, I did come," he insisted "You're just so out of it."

He then administered another dose of medication to me for the second time that morning. This should have been my third dose during his shift.

I remember thinking to myself, something is not adding up. So, after receiving my medication, he said to me, "now just lay and rest."

And that I finally did.

Shortly thereafter, no different than before, the same thing happened again. After about thirty or forty minutes the medicine stopped working. And I began to hurt. Knowing I had to wait for another two hours before I could get any help, I felt like I was reliving the previous episode—escalating pain with no relief. It was like I was trapped inside the whirlwind of a tornado.

Have you ever found yourself trapped in a wild spin that you couldn't control and each moment the rotation increased causing you more pain, anxiety, and frustration?

I consider Job who experienced a day when he heard one bad report after another—the loss of his donkeys, sheep, camels, sons, and daughters. All that he held so dearly was being snatched away from him—swallowed up and destroyed.

Job began to question God as he, just like I, felt abandoned. When things seemed to be at their worse, God answered Job's accusations. For God was in control and always remained in control. Just as He had done before, He sustained Job.

"Then the Lord answered Job out of the whirlwind, and said...Where wast thou when I laid the foundations of the earth? declare, if thou hast understanding." Job 38:1,4 (KJV)

I was depending on my primary nurse to do right by me, but God was teaching me a lesson about depending on Him, the source of my total relief.

As long as you're trusting in a man, as long as you're trusting in a human source, even though they might be a channel that God will work through, they are not the answer.

When the three hours had elapsed, I pushed my call button again. At this point, when the nursing assistant would come in, he or she would take my blood pressure. My systolic numbers had gone from 150 up to 170. The diastolic number had gone from 105 up to 125…130. Because the pain was a stressor, it was driving my blood pressure up and up. My blood pressure had gotten so high until my body would just shake in the bed from the pain of the spasms. I was hurting so badly. Again I called for the nurse, and the same thing happened. It was a repeat performance. He did not show up.

Five minutes to fifteen minutes to thirty minutes to an hour to an hour and a half. No nurse.

However, thank God my parents, during this time, came to visit me. They were very disturbed finding me in such a crisis. I began to tell them that I was trying to reach the nurse and as I began to tell them what had happened, my mother said, "Uh huh."

She looked as though she was looking through the situation. Using her career experience as an LPN, it was obvious that she had tapped into something. However, at that moment I didn't know what she understood and frankly could not comprehend anything beyond my immediate need. She chose not to reveal to me her intuitive suspicion at this time, but rather she chose for herself and my dad to offer me words of comfort.

My parents left me in the room at separate times to look for the missing nurse. He told them he had been there and he had given me my medication.

Upon each of their returns, I explained that he had not given me the medication and that this happened earlier that day as well. My mother using wisdom said to me, "you need to keep a journal, a log and just write down when your nurses come in and what they are giving you." Have them to sign their names on the log whenever they give you the medication.

And so, I began to do that religiously and meticulously without fail. I began to document who entered my room, why they came and if medication was given, I would record the time, name, and dosage of what I was given. Most importantly, I had them to sign their names on the log. Some complied, but others were quite annoyed. Some simply refused, feeling this request added another step to their duties. However, in retrospect, this self-imposed task became, for me, a healthy therapeutic activity as it was a partial distraction from feeling so helpless into having a sense of control in what seemed my uncontrollable situation.

Later that day, following more episodes of missed doses, my wife and daughter came to visit. Because I was in such intense pain, I just wanted them to leave and go home because I didn't want them to see me in such misery. I was so bad off, and there was nothing that they could do to help me. They prayed with me, and I just trusted God to get me through.

WATCH and SEE

After visiting hours were over that night and everyone was gone, my nurse mysteriously reappeared. But this time, he fell across my bed on top of my legs. He was holding a syringe in his hand, with pills, as he fell. He was very high.

I began to realize what was going on—my primary nurse was taking my medication. Each time that he didn't show up, he was using. Then he would lie and say that he had given medicine to me. In effect, he would give me a dose, then after the next three hours he would take a dose. Then he would give me another dose (six hours later), and then he would take my next dose. He had schemed that because I was so sick, and because I was labeled as becoming psychotic from the pain, he could request to be assigned to me and feed his addiction.

For the first time, I realized that both my nurse and I were suffering from chronic pain. We were codependent upon each other to receive medication. I needed him to be assigned to me to give me my medication to ease my pain. He needed to be assigned to me to take my medication to try to relieve his pain. He like I was addicted. I wonder what pain he was medicating? What was the enemy that was inside of him that ripped through his very being like a spasm? Neither of us was totally dependent upon the Great Physician to relieve our pain. We were both caught up in a whirlwind of addiction, using a physical narcotic to fix an underlying spiritual need.

The Lord began to show me, that as bad as that pain was, "I can take you through. I will hold your hand. I will maintain your blood pressure. I can keep it from going higher than it should go. And when it gets to its highest point, I will keep you despite the increase. I will be your keeper. I will be your sustainer, your Lord and your God, for I have made a promise to you and I will fulfill it."

My praise takes me to God, but worship brings Him to me. I physically could not go to God, but when I begin to worship God, I call Him to me. He had instructed me in my first out of body experience, "when you get in trouble, call for help." I mistook the call for help as my call button in the hospital bed, and here again physical help was not accessible to me. I learned a vital lesson that day. When the winds blow, and the pain comes, worship and call Him for help. He will come to us when we can't get to Him.

The Lord taught me to not trust in men, or in chariots (Psalm 20:7), but to trust in Him, my sustainer, and my keeper.

I reported the nurse to my primary physician, Dr. Saunders who handled the situation in full. Whereas I blamed my nurse for taking advantage of me, many decades later, I find myself prompted to pray for him no matter where he is because he just like me needs the merciful Savior and Deliverer. I look back on our interaction understanding that God let him be my primary teacher and the lesson for that day was on codependency and addiction. Just as God reached me, I pray that God reached him.

The trial of my sickness was far from over, but I would use this experience to realize that though things would get worse, Jesus is the author and finisher of my faith. He would sustain me, and I can worship Him for that. Again, as He allowed me to be taught, I would learn to "Watch and See" with greater expectation.

Words of Wisdom to Readers

Prior to this point, I was dependent upon the nurse to administer the medication. My source of relief from my spasms and intense pain was my medication. When the pain would come, I would call the nurse. The nurse would respond, and I would settle for the momentary relief. However, God was teaching me a more in-depth and enduring revelation. He alone is my strength and shield. We should accept that natural means may facilitate temporary relief. Yet in our frail human tendency, we often panic when our pain intensifies. However, the source of ultimate relief and comfort from all pain comes from God, who may choose to operate through medical science. However, God ultimately is the source with or without the usage of medical support. He is the embodiment of peace. Therefore, when you cannot find relief in the natural, seek spiritual relief in His Word, holding fast to His promises. Through worship, let God hookup a direct line into you like an IV. Your comfort will be in knowing that whenever you call Him, He will supply all your needs.

I've found that journaling my experiences shows my attempts to fix my circumstances. Yet, when I reread my journals, God's faithful hand is evident. I can trace my testimony over time. This is essential as we may not recall details, but the words on the pages of the journal will verify that God has been faithful to His Word.

"Wherefore take unto you the whole armour of God, that ye may be able to withstand in the evil day, and having done all, to stand. Stand..." Ephesians 6:13-14 (KJV)

Chapter 6

ON A WALK WITH GOD

"Yea, though I walk through the valley of the shadow of death, I will fear no evil: for thou art with me; thy rod and thy staff they comfort me."
Psalm 23:4 (KJV)

Have you ever felt as if you took one step forward followed by three steps backwards? Has your outlook ever been clouded by disappointment after progress? These were the ebbs and flows of my journey. In the course of nine surgeries, many times after long hospital stays, I would recuperate at home and progress to the point of walking and driving. But the vestiges of my pre-surgery condition complicated my post-surgery independence. Seemingly, my progress was always shrouded by what ifs relating to fall risks, unexpected complications, and resuming normal activities too soon.

This day my wife was very concerned about me staying at home. The issue was that I didn't want to remain at home. I wanted to go out and drive. Technically, I could drive; however, I had begun to take my medication in larger doses. My wife was afraid that I would be driving under the influence of the medication and hurt someone or myself. As my primary caregiver, my wife constantly carried the concern of my well-being when we were together and when we were apart. She worked full-time, mothered my daughter, and cared for me too.

So, she tried to convince me to stay in the house and not to go out until she returned home from work. However, my leaving the house was because I was bored and wanted a change of scenery. Being able to drive was certainly an asset and a plus for me, yet it was so dangerous. It was dangerous because driving under the influence of medication can be like driving under the influence of alcohol.

Thus, when my wife realized that I was not being reasonable, she locked me in the house so that she could go to work. I was in the house, and I was very angry with her. I felt that she was being unfair and excessively limiting my freedom. However, a lot of my reasoning was irrational. It was the result of being overly medicated, and I was so out of touch with reality.

Pain that is extended over a long-term period can create irrational thinking, mental imbalance, erratic emotions, and just losing touch, period.

There I was locked in the house. I was extremely frustrated, and I just wanted to get out. Because my wife locked me inside, so that she could go to work and provide for us with a partial peace of mind for my safety, she needed to know that I was confined. The best place for me to be was at home.

Apparently, there was no one available at that time that could sit with me or perhaps even I didn't want a sitter. I would go in and out of that whole ego thing, and I wanted my independence. Some of that was a result of long-term inpatient hospital stays or being in the bed, on my back, unable to move about. So, then when I got the freedom and when I got the ability, I didn't want any restrictions.

There I was, locked in the house behind a wrought iron storm door. I then went on a maneuver, a manhunt looking for another set of keys to unlock the door. I searched, and searched, and searched, and searched and, somehow, I found a spare key.

When I found the spare key, I then decided to leave the house. I didn't have a car to drive because my wife drove the car to work. I concluded that I didn't need a car because I could walk. I packed my bag with all my medications: Valium, Vistaril, Tylenol with Codeine, Dilaudid, Halcion, Flexeril, and Soma. I packed all my muscle relaxers and pain killers and hallucinogens into a bag, after I had taken (only God knows how many pills). No food, clothes, or water made it into my bag, just my medications that would have been worth thousands of dollars on the street. I decided that I was going to walk to my parents' house.

Now, I should state that by car, my parents' house was a fifteen minute ride using major streets that became progressively hilly. My wife and I lived in a small suburb on the edge of the city. My parents lived further away from the city in a larger suburb. This was a little more than five miles door to door.

I was so high from my medications until I barely remember leaving my house. All that I know is that I would hear car horns blowing. I would look up and the traffic was stopped because I was walking in the street. I remember vaguely crossing Liberty Road, a major four lane street during mid-day, and there was traffic everywhere.

I remember leaning up against a telephone poll and then waking up saying to myself, "What am I doing?" I remember trying to walk normally and not appear as though I was going to fall. I remember walking down the street, and I saw a lady who was selling blueberries and plums at a make-shift fruit stand on the sidewalk in front of her home. I decided that I wanted some. I could tell that the lady was frightened by my appearance as I approached her, and she jumped, but offered me free fruit.

She said to me, "You can have whatever you want."

I must have looked intoxicated, high, and crazy.

I said to her, "I just want to buy some fruit." I handed her my money (only she knows how much I gave her). She gave me a bag of fruit. I continued to walk until I reached my parents' door.

I rang the doorbell. I remember my mother opening the door and grabbing me. She hugged me and began to cry. I remember her asking me, "Where in the world have you been? We've been calling the house trying to find you. Ronaé has been looking for you, and she's worried sick."

I came into the house, and I lay down. I had walked for three hours from our house to my parents' house—a trip that takes only fifteen minutes by car, and about an hour for a healthy person to walk. According to my family, I slept for several hours after that.

Well, many days later, my wife took me to the doctor, and he reported a startling fact. If I had not gone for a three hour walk, I would have overdosed on my medication at home.

God took me for a walk, and the scripture that comes to my mind is Genesis 5:24 which describes Enoch as he walked with God. You might say, but Enoch was in right relationship with God. Yes, that is true. However, I walked with God by grace and mercy, not because I earned the right to receive it, but by God's goodness and mercy. He gave it freely. "Surely goodness and mercy shall follow me all the days of my life: and I will dwell in the house of the Lord for ever." Psalm 23:6 (KJV)

God kept me and preserved me and protected me from myself and others who could have harmed me.

Nevertheless, I walked with God. Despite me, despite my predicament, the Lord preserved me and protected me.

Therefore, when I remember that day, and the major streets and intersections I crossed, on my walk with God, the experience is forever etched in my mind like a stone memorial.

"Then Samuel took a stone...and called the name of it Ebenezer, saying, Hitherto hath the Lord helped us." 1 Samuel 7:12 (KJV)

Words of Wisdom to Readers

Whether we are praying for someone else, as my wife and parents prayed for me, or whether someone needs prayer, as I needed, God can walk anyone through the valley of the shadow of death. God can keep anyone alive in the

MARCUS A. JOHNSON, SR.

valley of the shadow of death. We are all imperfect testimonies in the making, being transformed by God's mercy and His grace.

When we find ourselves desperate to be freed from our circumstantial confinement, even stepping into self-imposed new dangers, we need to walk with God. He is the only Good Shepherd that can lead us into green pastures and beside still waters. He alone can restore our souls. In this life, we must learn to walk with God.

Chapter 7

A STRANGE PLACE TO BE

"Fear thou not; for I am with thee: be not dismayed; for I am thy God: I will strengthen thee; yea, I will help thee; yea, I will uphold thee with the right hand of my righteousness."
Isaiah 41:10 (KJV)

One of my most horrendous experiences among so many happened when I was an inpatient in Hospital A. There I was in so much pain. This was around my sixth surgery and the truth was that I really wasn't getting any better.

I was told that I would improve, but I wasn't. Prior to my accident on February 22, 1983, I had never had a surgery except a double hernia operation that occurred when I was a very young child, according to my parents. I was so young until I have no recollection of this experience.

Here I am, six surgeries later and I didn't know that an unfortunate experience on one day would last this long. At this point, I existed in a brand-new body cast that stretched from my mid-chest to just below my knees. The cast was to keep me immobile so that my body could properly heal from the surgery. Indeed, I was very uncomfortable in this body cast. I used crutches to ambulate very short distances, but I required assistance to use steps, go to the bathroom, bathe, or to get in and out of the bed.

The doctor began expressing concerns about all of the medication that I was taking. He said, "We need to consider putting you in a pain management program." He recommended the program (clinic) in Maryland where the specialist, on staff at Hospital D, ran the program. He concluded by saying, "I'd like to have you transferred there."

As I consented, I thought that perhaps this would lead to an improvement in my condition over the next few months. I was transferred via ambulance to the clinic. The strangest thing happened when I arrived. A member of the clinic's staff led the paramedics up to my room located on the second floor. The clinic appeared to be a very old, huge mansion. The facility was so large and the rooms were huge and the ceilings were very high. I was told that in the morning that they would begin my treatment program. Certainly, I just didn't know what to expect.

On that evening, my wife and my daughter came to visit me. While my wife talked with the manager of the facility, I was very mindful of my discomfort in this new place while wearing this brand-new body cast. Because I wanted my wife to be encouraged in such a hellish situation, it became a practice that I often wouldn't share with her the details of what I was feeling and thinking in an attempt to normalize a very abnormal phenomenon. Despite my best efforts to conceal my pain, my wife was very perceptive. This is part of her nature and to this day, she always knows when things are right and more importantly, when they are not.

As the three of us began to pray, I, my wife, and my daughter, I grappled with the reality that I was going to be left alone in this strange place. Unlike being at home with family, or in the hospital filled with staff and patients, this place was remote, cold, dark, and lonely. It reminded me of a haunted house where the unknown lurks in the quiet darkness.

My daughter could not have been more than five years old at that time. As we prayed, I desperately wanted to say, "Don't leave me here." But as the man, the husband, and the father, I wouldn't tell them how I really felt. But I was afraid! Even if I chose to leave without the assistance of paramedics or staff, there was no way my wife could have gotten me out of this facility to transport me anywhere. It was physically impossible for her to accomplish such a feat.

After they left, there I was in this huge place. Earlier that day, I was told by a member of the clinic's staff that there would be workers there at all times. During the night, the attendant appeared from out of nowhere. He gave me his name and said that he had come just to check on me. He told me if I needed help to just yell for him and he would come. "Yell," he said. This meant I would have to scream loudly, sending a frightening echo through the heavy air in the mansion, and then wait for someone to appear in my doorway. This entire predicament was eerily spooky. There I was in the room, alone, in my body cast with my crutches.

In the morning a greater problem was apparent. Once the attendant assisted me into the bathroom, I realized that there was a small hole in the back of my cast to allow me to sit on the commode and relieve myself. The cast was so poorly designed until I was unable to get into a seated position. This cast was hurriedly fitted just before I was transferred, and I hadn't had the opportunity to test its functionality using the commode. As a matter of fact, it had been many hours since I had used a commode prior to being fitted for this cast. Honestly, a horrendous side effect of my medications was constipation. Soon, I discovered the unthinkable—I couldn't position myself adequately to use the commode or bed pan. This meant that I couldn't go to the bathroom. But that night, I had to make a conscious decision, to override my misery and wait until the following morning, alone, in my body cast. Besides, I didn't want to keep yelling for the attendant who appeared to sleepwalk when I called him.

Let me take this time to insert a necessary thought to those who may feel these details are quite trivial. Using the bathroom, a very normal everyday practice is not a big deal until you can't go due to constipation or other technical difficulties. It's then that a small thing becomes a monumental thing. What we typically take for granted becomes most appreciated when it's not doable.

However, with so much pain in my body, reposing in this big mansion and big room was difficult. The night seemed so black. I began to yell for the attendant to come and assist me so that I could use the bathroom. My stomach was upset, and I needed to relieve myself. I thought maybe he could cut a hole in the bottom of the cast or do something to increase the size of the opening.

Ironically, for some people who are ill and so dependent on another to help them physically, their intact mind incessantly calculates how to perform a needed task. I spent so much time thinking and reasoning. I would often map out a plan in my mind first and then call for help so that I could explain exactly what I needed and how the help of another person would create the solution that I needed. I already felt like I was being a disturbance and I feared total rejection and maybe even retribution.

Nevertheless, I yelled, and I yelled, and I yelled, and no one came all night. I began to wonder, if anyone was in the facility with me. Could I have been there all by myself? In the 1980's there were no cell phones or tablets in wide use. I couldn't tweet my wife, or post a photo with an SOS call for help on Instagram.

No one came all night. In the black of night, I stared at the darkness as if the darkness had a face. I said, "Lord, if you don't keep me, I won't make it."

I began to remember the scripture, "I will never leave thee, nor forsake thee." Hebrews 13:5 (KJV) And even though I felt alone and forsaken, that night I learned peace in knowing that God is always there and that God sees, and He hears, and He cares. That night, I was lying there in that bed, unable to relieve myself, in so much misery, alone with God, facing the darkness, just me, and my body cast and my crutches.

I knew that I dare not attempt to get up alone because if I fell, who would help me. I would have been stranded endlessly on the cold floor, in this remote, cold, dark, and lonely place.

In the morning, as I heard staff filling the mansion downstairs, a nurse came into my room. She assessed that I did in fact need a larger hole to be cut into the cast. My mind trailed off as I remembered the first making of the body cast. It was difficult and uncomfortable. Yet, the needed modifications were necessary.

This encounter taught me once again that you can't put confidence in man alone. The Bible says, "in all thy ways acknowledge Him, and He shall direct thy paths." Proverbs 3:6 (KJV)

I want to tell you that God kept me, and He sustained me in that lonely, destitute, and difficult situation. When you are alone and stuck in a situation with no way out, with God you can face the darkness. Use your confidence in God, even if it seems inadequate, and find comfort. Let God be faithful, even in the dark, even in an unfamiliar place because He is the God of the darkness as well as the light.

Words of Wisdom to Readers

There is purpose in every situation that may not appear obvious. But nothing can happen to a believer except God allows it to happen. Moreover, it is in these impossible times, where we are left all alone in the dark, that true purpose is revealed. The Lord wants you to know that He is our light. He is our crutch to lean upon. He is our dependable companion who never sleeps or slumbers. Know that He will make a way for our relief through His grace. It is in these strange places that God teaches us not to be afraid.

"For I the Lord thy God will hold thy right hand, saying unto thee, Fear not; I will help thee." Isaiah 41:13 (KJV)

Chapter 8

RIGHT ON THE VERGE

*"And Joshua rose early in the morning; and they removed
from Shittim, and came to Jordan, he and all the children of
Israel, and lodged there before they passed over."*
Joshua 3:1 (KJV)

Upon being discharged from the clinic, I began to reflect on my first group session that I attended at that location. The background that you need to know is that many patients were admitted into the clinic, during my stay, and we were instructed to enter a large living room for psychoanalysis. I had never been exposed to anything like this before.

Hence, in this large room, we sat in a circle and the doctor, who sat at the head of the circle, instructed each patient to share his or her story with the group. He encouraged us to tell what had happened that caused us to be in that facility. For some reason or another, he told me to start.

I remember feeling shy and very reticent because I didn't fully understand this type of program. I was in a lot of pain. Living with chronic pain had become my reality. There were others around me who also suffered, on some level. We were all hurting. Most of us managed our pain with heavy narcotics. I wondered, why I was chosen to start this exercise. But to be cooperative, I asked him, "Exactly what do you want me to share?"

He said, "Tell us your story. Tell us what happened to you. Tell us how you got here."

I started off by saying my name. I remember explaining that I had an accident on my job on February 22, 1983. I talked about the sheetrock falling on me and the extensive damage that I had sustained in my body and specifically my spine. I explained the resultant effects on my nervous system and how the nerves in my

MARCUS A. JOHNSON, SR.

back malfunction which causes chronic pain. I expressed how a spasm will occur and shake my body, and it is just so painful.

I am not sure how long I spoke, but I recall trying to be descriptive as I felt myself really opening up. Then I happened to notice that the doctor, who had been writing as I was speaking, had put down his pen and paper. He had perched his hands in midair over his shoulder, and he pretended to be playing an invisible violin.

I was baffled, so I stopped talking in mid-sentence as suddenly everything in the moment stopped making sense. I could feel everything all at once; my cast, the chair, the air in the room, everything was thick and hard and very heavy.

The doctor responded, "Oh excuse me, go ahead and keep telling your story."

Reluctantly, I resumed talking this time with my eyes glued to the doctor. I noticed again that he in fact was pretending to play an air violin. But this time, he added the sound of music, imitating the whining pitch of a bow sliding across the violin strings.

I stopped again. This time I was getting angry, and I was very guarded. I began to realize that he was making fun of me as if to say, you are telling such a sad story, so let me give you some sad, background, mood music. Let me provide the accompaniment to your dramatic story, as if I were on stage in a theater telling a whining tale.

Everything about him, from his gaze, to the tone of his voice, to the patronizing motion of his arms, was done to make fun of me. I remember I looked at him and said, "I resent your reaction with all the pain that I'm in and all the difficultly that I've experienced. I resent the fact that you would sit here, ask me to tell why I'm here and then make fun of me like that. I will not sit here and tolerate this."

I was outraged.

I felt INSULTED—I WAS LIVID!

Then he said to me very coolly, "Well you're telling a dramatic story. If you want to be dramatic, I want you to have the proper backdrop."

He went on to address the entire group who appeared frightened and appalled on my behalf. "What I want all of you to understand is that you have allowed your conditions to become the focal point of your lives. You have allowed your pain and your difficulty to become the dominant theme of wherever you go. You have subjected your family and your friends and everyone else to what you are going through. And part of this program's purpose is to teach you to stop being the center of your world."

I was shocked. I was astounded because I had been tricked, duped, hoodwinked, and sucker punched. I was embarrassed and felt like a prop on the stage of this doctor's theater. If we were in the middle of a performance, all I wanted was an intermission. I desperately wanted a break, not just from the scene that we were in, but from life.

God, please make it stop.

I remember the hot tears welling up in my eyes. I looked around at the other patients who were still apparently in shock themselves. Some of them began to cry.

When I would have further defended myself, I could hear a voice in my heart. It was faint but it was true.

"Thou shall have no other gods before me." Exodus 20:3 (KJV)

"Thou shalt worship the Lord thy God, and him only shalt thou serve." Matthew 4:10 (KJV)

"God is a Spirit: and they that worship him must worship him in spirit and in truth." John 4:24 (KJV)

I began to cry, not because of the words of the doctor leading the group, but I was convicted. As I wept, I realized that I had allowed my condition; my predicament; and my circumstances to become my life's theme song. I had allowed what I was going through to trump everything else. My pain had become the object of my worship. It was my god.

In that humiliating moment, I made a conscious decision that I would choose never again to dwell and be fixated on my circumstances. In the words of Job I declared in my heart, "Though he slay me, yet will I trust in him...all the days of my appointed time will I wait, till my change come." Job 13:15 and 14:14 (KJV)

Job remarks, "...the Lord gave, and the Lord hath taken away; blessed be the name of the Lord." Job 1:21 (KJV)

God must be my theme song. He must be the focal point. I had learned then that I must worship God and God alone. This awareness became a constant pulse that coursed rhythmically through my veins and persisted for the duration of my illness.

The scripture says, "Thou wilt keep him in perfect peace, whose mind is stayed on thee: because he trusteth in thee." Isaiah 26:3 (KJV)

I thank God for that physician and his violin. Unknowingly, he taught me that in my drama, Jesus Christ must always and preeminently take center stage.

I realized, just like Joshua and the Children of Israel, that I could not defeat the Canaanites in my promised land until I crossed my Jordan River. I had to leave the power that my pain had over me behind me in order to enter my promised land. Then and only then could I discover the purpose of my pain—it's a bridge to true victory and true worship. But I had to choose not to remain on the verge and cross over. God is faithful. He had preserved me from destruction in captivity, and He would lead me from this precipice into victory.

Words of Wisdom to Readers

This chapter teaches a vital life lesson. True worship precedes true victory. True worship can only take place after getting to the Jordan River,

a defining location that separates our captivity and wanderings from our promised land.

For it was after Joshua led Israel across the Jordan River in a processional following the priest with the Ark of the Covenant that they camped in Gilgal, renewed their covenant with God, and worshipped Him there. This true worship became the qualifier of their true victories.

If we allow the sufferings, disappointments, frustrations, and past defeats to remain our focal point and preoccupation, we practice idolatry and false worship. Only defeat will proceed from idolatry and false worship. However, we can change course and follow God's presence. We can cross over our Jordan River and enter our land of promise where we can worship the true promise keeper, who will enable our victory.

Chapter 9

A WAY OF ESCAPE

"There hath no temptation taken you but such as is common to man: but God is faithful, who will not suffer you to be tempted above that ye are able; but will with the temptation also make a way to escape, that ye may be able to bear it."
1 Corinthians 10:13 (KJV)

I remember it well that after my sixth surgery at a local hospital (Hospital C), I was lying in my bed. At that time, I shared a room with another young man and he was also very ill. Like me, my roommate had an orthopedic surgery to correct a spinal injury. He was also confined to his bed.

This was a classic God setup—neither of us could walk without assistance. This was an opportunity to share the gospel of Jesus Christ. I would talk about the goodness of the Lord and God's faithfulness during the aftermath of my accident on February 22. Often, God will assign us to a situation to minister to someone else. "Let your light so shine before men, that they may see your good works, and glorify your father which is in Heaven." Matthew 5:16 (KJV)

As my visitors would come in the room to see me, I would share those moments with my roommate, also, partly because the room was so small and because I knew that he appreciated hearing the encouragement. Everyone needs to be encouraged at some point in time. This young man was just very comforted and uplifted by the love that my visitors would show to him.

Being a witness was a mainstay of my roommate experiences throughout the nine major surgeries and my multiple hospital visits. My immediate roommate usually enjoyed my visitors. It was as though we were related, and my relatives were family to him and vice versa.

Visiting hours were now over and I rested in my room, talking to my roommate; we were having a very normal and casual conversation. Suddenly, there was a major loud explosion in the hospital. We didn't know from where it emanated, but the force shook the room. It shook the room so violently until some things fell to the floor. Almost in unison my roommate and I screamed aloud, "What was that? What was that?"

For two patients, unable to walk without assistance post-surgery, we were instantly, and without warning, in a helpless situation. We lay there with no information, or updates, and no way to get up.

It is so hard to describe the helplessness that you feel when you are sick and you cannot do for yourself. When anything occurs that breaks the normalcy of your routine, there is a crushing fear that occurs because you know that you are dependent on someone else for help. Obviously, had we been able to walk, we would have run to the door and out of the room.

As my roommate began to cry and to yell, the reality of the moment and my assignment flooded my mind. If we were going to die then this moment would be eternally significant. If we were going to be rescued then this moment could become a defining moment for my roommate. Everything that I had shared with my roommate on good days, when there was no imminent danger, was relevant right now. This was a God given opportunity for me to demonstrate the truth of God's Word. "God is our refuge and strength, a very present help in trouble." Psalm 46:1 (KJV)

I began to comfort him and assure him that everything was going to be alright and that the Lord was going to provide for us a way of escape. We began to hear and see the medical staff running up and down the hallway. There was a noxious gas smell. Then I could see that the gas vapor was entering the room. We didn't know what we were breathing, nor did we understand what was happening. The white vapor was filling the room like a wispy cloud.

A nurse slammed the door of our room and left us inside. And we could hear so many footsteps racing up and down the hallway. We were shouting, "What's going on? What's going on? Can somebody help us?"

It seemed like hours had passed before someone opened the door. In the distance, we could just see the nurses rolling patients in their beds down the hallway. As the gas was getting stronger and stronger, my roommate became increasingly frightened. Even though I was afraid, my calm came from the scriptures that I was rehearsing in my head. Let me be very clear; I too was terrified. This was an extraordinarily scary experience, but I knew that if I became hysterical I wouldn't have the presence of mind that was needed in this crisis.

I began to say the scriptures in my head, aloud, and my roommate began to respond and repeat the words that I was saying. I knew that he didn't know the Lord for himself, but he was grabbing onto my faith. I began to realize that he was dependent upon my prayers, my faith, and my peace. He was taking comfort from my comfort with God. All I had to draw from were scriptures that were coming to my mind. I continued to minister to him and to myself in the atmosphere of intense panic.

"He that dwelleth in the secret place of the most High shall abide under the shadow of the Almighty...Thou shalt not be afraid for the terror by night; nor for the arrow that flieth by day; Nor for the pestilence that walketh in darkness; nor for the destruction that wasteth at noonday." Psalm 91:1,5,6 (KJV)

I was amazed that I could remember these scriptures. I didn't really know that I had memorized them. But this Word was hidden deep in my heart, and the Word was calming my fears. I felt my faith rising as another scripture came to mind.

"...but God is faithful, who will not suffer you to be tempted above that ye are able; but will with the temptation also make a way to escape, that ye may be able to bear it." 1 Corinthians 10:13 (KJV)

But gas was steadily building up in the room, and we both began to cough and to choke. Finally, a nurse came to assure us we were not forgotten, as the nurses were running up and down the hall, back and forth, screaming instructions. It was clear that this was an evacuation. We had never seen children on our floor, but patients of all types were whizzing past our now open door.

The scene was so strange and very surreal.

Another nurse appeared in our doorway and said, "We are going to get to you soon. We are trying to evacuate those on the second floor and those who are in the basement. You two are closest to the exit because this is the first floor. I promise we will get you out. Be patient and be calm; we are going to get you out."

With that brief burst of information, the nurse turned on her heels to run back into the hallway.

We yelled, "What is happening?"

She said, "I can't talk right now." In a flash, she was gone. She dashed into the hallway, and we could hear her footsteps disappear into the cacophony of hysteria all around us. Thank God I used this time to pray directly with and for my roommate. He gladly received this prayer. It was as though God had primed him for this very hour.

It is important to be a living witness for God. It is through consistency on good days and bad days that we shine the light of Christ upon those who are lost, hurting, sick, and lonely. Overtime, they learn through our witness that the source of their help comes from God. Therefore, when a defining moment comes, the lost, hurting, sick, and lonely have already been introduced to the love and ways of God through a consistent witness. This helps to create room for faith.

I just cannot remember how long we waited. It is common to think that one minute or even five minutes is an hour when you're in the middle of acutely fierce and overwhelming crisis.

I do remember that we looked out of our window as we began to hear sirens and then more sirens. Layered on top of the noise, we began to see fire engines. Then we saw the firemen running into the hospital with their equipment entering our hallway. They were running past our door, and someone ducked their head into our room quickly and asked, "Are you okay?"

We responded, "we're okay but please help us, please don't forget us, we can't walk without assistance."

I don't know how long it took for them to get to us, but finally they came for us; it was our turn. I said to the nurse, "take my roommate first. Take him first."

She nodded, rolling my roommate out. Almost immediately, another nurse came for me and rolled my entire bed out of the room. Finally, I was rescued, leaving the smoke-filled room, surging into the hallway.

I was rolled outside onto the lawn. Seeing so many beds surrounding me, it was obvious that the entire hospital had been emptied. All the beds were outside on the lawn. I had never seen anything like this before. There was a sea of hospital beds, wheelchairs, and all sorts of equipment on that lawn. I saw adult and pediatric patients. We were packed on the lawn as if it were a parking lot. I could barely see the green grass beneath us. The hospital lawn looked like pure mayhem.

Finally, a reporter walked over to me and asked me for my name. He then proceeded, "Mr. Johnson do you know what has just happened?" I could barely find my voice as I responded, "No."

He said, the boiler exploded in the hospital and poisonous gases were escaping. He asked, "How do you feel?"

As I drank in the reality of his words which were easily confirmed by the swirling images of patients all around me on the lawn, I screamed, "I feel blessed, I feel relieved that I got out of there...and it was a frightening experience, and...I just want to go home. I want to go home."

Someone approached me from behind, and my bed began moving. I could see that I was being wheeled to another area on the lawn; as it appeared that the workers were trying to group the patients, but by what criteria I did not know.

I looked over, and it was clear what God was showing me in this situation.

There was a little child. While I could not determine her age exactly, I would guess that she was eight or nine years old. She had no legs or arms. She was propped up on a pillow, and she was in what looked like a bed on wheels with bars on all four sides. I gazed further and saw more children who were without limbs and with deformities in their facial form. I was clear that they had been brought out of the pediatric area of the hospital.

As I brought my gaze back to the first little girl, I could see that she was laughing and singing.

And the Lord began to say to me, "If she can laugh, if she can experience joy during all of this, how much more should you?"

I began to realize that no matter what condition I'm in, my response should always be to give thanks. "In everything give thanks: for this is the will of God in Christ Jesus, concerning you." 1 Thessalonians 5:18 (KJV)

As dangerous and intensely emotional as this experience was, God kept his promise to me. There is always a way of escape.

Words of Wisdom to Readers

The Lord will allow what appears to be our misfortune or disadvantage to become a divine assignment. Ultimately, what we labeled an accident may really be a divine ministry opportunity in the making. This is a practical example of giving thanks to God while in a bad situation. Thanksgiving can change your perspective on a bad thing. There is transforming power in a grateful heart.

In the words of Joseph, "...ye thought evil against me; but God meant it unto good, to bring to pass, as it is this day, to save much people alive." Genesis 50:20 (KJV)

We must learn to be opportunity seizers—when misfortune comes, be a witness for Christ, wherever we find ourselves. Often, after we have shared our faith, what would appear to be a great problem becomes a stage to demonstrate our true faith.

In this case, talk is cheap except when it is lived out in real time. As sinners and even weaker believers react to their circumstances in fear, frustration, and doubt, it is incumbent on us, as true believers, and true witnesses, to model our faith before them.

"...for my strength is made perfect in weakness. Most gladly therefore will I rather glory in my infirmities, that the power of Christ may rest upon me." 2 Corinthians 12:9 (KJV)

Remember, whenever we find ourselves trapped in circumstances, God has provided strength in his Word. There is always a way of escape.

Chapter 10

GOD IS WAITING FOR THE PERFECT MOMENT

> *"And the Lord appointed a set time, saying, To morrow the Lord shall do this thing in the land."*
> *Exodus 9:5 (KJV)*

As you consider your circumstances and read about my own, the question may occur to you, "so what is God waiting for?" I want God to move on my behalf. After all, He desires to move. He exists to manifest His glory in us. But remember, He is perfect and we are not. God waits for perfect alignment between His word, our faith, and the appointed time. There is even a set moment at the appointed time, prescheduled before the foundation of the world. Only God can judge that moment. His watch keeps perfect time, with no minutes or seconds wasted. God is waiting for the perfect moment.

I awakened this morning, in 1989, no differently than any morning before. I was lying in my bed in Hospital D. Because I was paralyzed, I learned how to improvise. I could bathe myself and get ready for the day when my so-called tools were in place.

I would start with my reacher (an assistive reaching device) and lift the plastic basin off the counter. Next, I would put the basin on the portable tray positioned on wheels and push the tray to the sink with the basin positioned under the water spout. I would turn the water on and fill the basin. Then with my reacher, I turned the water off at the sink and then pulled the tray back toward my bed. This was a precise maneuver that I learned how to perform through trial and error, knowing how much water to use, how much weight the tray could withstand, and how much strength to exert to push and pull the tray.

MARCUS A. JOHNSON, SR.

With this accomplished, I began to bathe myself before the morning nurse arrived. There was a trapeze apparatus overhead, attached to my bedframe, which I used to pull myself up off the mattress. Because I could not use my legs, I learned to use my arms and perform all sorts of maneuvers. I could raise myself, and gather the sheet as well as the blanket on the mattress beneath me.

It was very important to my self-confidence that I could maintain a level of independence. I simply could not open my eyes day after day knowing that I relied on everyone for everything when I had some ability through skilled maneuvers. In my own way, being able to bathe myself, make my bed, and be ready for breakfast was preeminent. I knew the nurses would arrive in my room by 7am for the morning check-in as the shifts changed. Therefore, it was important to me that when they arrived, everything concerning my hygiene was already completed. I had maintained my privacy and preserved what remained as my personal dignity.

Like always, the nurses applauded my ingenuity and the morning began.

But this morning was unique. I heard God speaking to me in my spirit. He said, "Today you will preach your first sermon in this hospital."

And I asked the Lord, "How am I going to do that, I'm paralyzed, I'm bedridden?"

And the Lord said, "I will provide the audience."

Not soon after, the nurse entered my room and said, "Mr. Johnson this morning the doctors want to see the patients in the pain treatment program in the conference room, one at a time."

Immediately, I knew that this was the Lord's provision for my audience. What I would say and what I would do; I did not know. Nevertheless, I was confident that just as he allowed me to bathe myself and make my bed, he would provide whatever I needed in this assignment as well.

All the patients were gathered in the reception area; as we were told, we would be called into the conference room, one at a time. The patients were very uneasy, and some were very annoyed, as this was quite different from our normal routine and daily experience. It was the norm that throughout the day we would sit in groups to complete activities and discussions. Sometimes, we filled out forms, and completed other tasks. We were called together and told that we would be separated to go before the medical staff. I was the only patient who was in a wheelchair. The rest of the patients suffered from other ailments, but they could mobilize and walk. The Lord arranged that of the fifteen patients, the nurses chose me to be the last one to go before the medical team.

I sat in my wheelchair and waited for my turn. I watched the patients go into the conference room, one at a time, and come out crying, screaming with their heads down, appearing very upset and depressed. Some came out muttering to themselves, which only upset the other patients waiting to go in. However, there was such an unusual peace and a calm that had come over me. I was not nervous or afraid. I knew that God had arranged this for me to preach my first sermon in the hospital today. As I sat there, I didn't have anything prepared in my thoughts. I trusted God to give me what to say.

The nurse said to me, "Mr. Johnson it is now your turn. Let me wheel you into the room."

But, I heard the Lord say, "Don't allow anyone to take charge. You show the initiative. Open your mouth, and I will fill it with what to say."

So, I obeyed and took the initiative. I said to the nurse, "No thank you. I'll wheel myself in."

So, she opened the door, and I wheeled myself into the center of the room where fourteen doctors and nurses were seated in a semi-circle wearing white lab coats. I felt intimidated. It was as if they were looking through me. Their pads and pencils were ready, and they seemed eager to begin their inquisition.

I felt the confidence of God sweeping over me. I opened my mouth and said, "Good morning everybody, my name is Marcus Johnson. I have a few things I want to say to you and then I will be out of your way."

I saw the shock on their faces because they had called me into the room, but God was leading me to officiate at this meeting. That's right, I was officiating at the meeting they called. God was in charge.

The head doctor responded, "Mr. Johnson, we called you into this room."

And I proceeded to talk as though I didn't even hear what he had said.

I continued, "When I came to this hospital, I thought I was coming here for you to fix me, and the Lord reminded me that at the scene of the accident in Westview Mall and Hospital A, after my second surgery that I had two out of body experiences, respectively. At that hospital, my spirit was in the ceiling with God while my lifeless body lay upon the bed. There was nothing wrong with my spirit, but there was something wrong with the physical house that I lived in. Thus, I have come to this hospital to allow the Lord to fix my physical house. Meanwhile, I will continue to occupy it during the reconstruction and the renovation processes."

One of the doctors asked, "What are you talking about?"

And I said to her, "I am sharing with you what my new assignment here is about." They all looked baffled and very confused.

One of the doctors asked, "How are you going to manage the pain that you're in?"

I responded, "Oh that, now that I know the spasms from the renovations are causing the pain, when it comes I'll simply brace myself and deal with it."

So, another doctor asked, "What about the very traumatic spasms that you have? How are you going to deal with that?"

I answered, "Now that I know that my old house doesn't have a driveway, but my new house will, I now understand that the spasms are caused by the construction workers jack hammering through the concrete to install the driveway. When they

63

are doing the heavy-duty work, it causes me to have heavy duty spasms. So, I will just go upstairs as they continue to work, and we will fellowship together."

And several members of the team asked simultaneously, "Who are the we?"

And I said, "My Lord and me. We walk together. We talk to together."

Then I proceeded to share that when I came to this hospital, I was like a ship that had been tormented at sea and for fear of drowning, I took my ship out of the water and placed it on dry ground. I now know that a ship was never intended to be on dry ground. Therefore, I am taking my ship and putting it back in the sea. I'm taking the water out of the ship so that I can set sail. They looked at me with amazement and astonishment as I proceeded to give them an insight into what the Lord was doing in my life.

I said to them, "Despite your medical report and what you have found, before your very eyes I am going to get up and walk again. Therefore, contrary to what you have said, I will not die. I am going to live. You don't have to believe what I'm saying, just Watch and See. Have a great day everybody because I already am. God bless you."

Immediately, I grabbed the wheels of my chair and turned the wheelchair around. The doctors and nurses, amazed, stood in a standing ovation, and with applause at my back I left the room. They had forgotten that their role was to probe and question me to evoke a raw reaction for their research. Yet, so quickly they had been swept up into a moment of great expectation that God was about to do something. I wheeled myself around and exited the room on my own while listening to the applause as I rolled down the hall. No one followed me. No one came after me. I went directly to my room, alone.

The air was pregnant with expectation. My faith had been elevated. My confidence was high. I was paralyzed, but knew I was approaching a miracle. God had a perfect time planned.

Two hours later, the pain group gathered in physical therapy where we would go through our daily routines and exercises. The only thing that I could do was to allow the nurse to lay me on the physical therapy table. There, I watched the other patients perform their routines and exercises. The room was windowless and carpeted. It was well lit and large containing all kinds of physical therapy equipment including tables, exercise bikes, and weight stacks with pulleys. I remember the patients were seated throughout the room. Although I couldn't do much, we were kept together as a group. We all went to physical therapy together.

Normally, I would become depressed and disenchanted as I watched the other patients do what I could not do in therapy. I was not able to move beyond certain positions because I could bring on a major spasmodic attack. But this time, there was such a peace that came over me that I was not disturbed.

Then again, the Lord spoke to me in my spirit and said, "Marcus, you have been obedient and you have done what I told you to do. Now it's time for you to

WATCH and SEE

walk." Mind you, this was not an audible voice, but a voice that pressed upon my thoughts as it emanated from my inner spirit.

And I asked the Lord, "How are we going to do it?"

The Lord said, "Have the nurse take you to the parallel bars; that's where we're going to walk."

And so, I beckoned for the nurse to come to me and she did. I said to her, "I need to go to the parallel bars because I am getting ready to walk."

She threw her hands over her eyes and began to shake her head, "No, no, no Mr. Johnson," she replied. "I cannot let you do that. If you fall you will die right here."

It was obvious, to me, that she was so traumatized by my announcement that she had become overwhelmed because it was clear to her that I was determined to attempt what I had said. Any other nurse would have just walked away; would have just thrown her hands up and passively said, "whatever". But this nurse heard the authority of God in my voice. With all of her ambivalence, she knew that these instructions were different. How and what she would do, she could not have known.

A spirit of righteous indignation came over me. By faith I could sense that something different was occurring. I couldn't let her fear interrupt this moment. I pointed my finger at her and demanded, "In the name of Jesus Christ, take me to those parallel bars."

As though God had snatched her, she reached under me, and lifted me to the edge of the table. I was steadily pulling myself using the adjoining railing. At the edge of the table, the nurse lifted me into the wheelchair. She moved mechanically, trance like, rolling me to the parallel bars.

There was a profound and dense silence in the room. Normally, the room would have been filled with the urging of physical therapists, instructing patients, or the groans of patients performing exercises, but not now. There were no shrieks or gasps. I heard deafening silence. I knew everyone in the room was watching. After all, I was a member of the group that just laid on the table and watched everyone else, but today they were motionless and watching me. I was totally caught up in the moment. It was as if I was having a vision.

After getting me to the parallel bars the nurse suggested frantically, "Please, let me help you get up."

I raised my hands towards her saying, "Back up, I'm getting ready to walk."

She backed up, looking at me saying, "Oh my God."

She was shaking from head to toe. I noticed that the patients in the room had stopped exercising and were watching. These very patients had not socialized or spoken to me previously because they felt they could not relate to me. I was the only young, Black, paralyzed patient in the program. They observed me from afar, but this time they were all focused upon what was about to take place.

I dropped my head, and I began to pray.

"Father in the name of Jesus, I have done what you said. And now the eyes of this hospital are upon you. On the count of three, let me get up and walk."

Then I lifted my head, wiped the tears from my eyes, and I announced to the room, "On the count of three, I'm going to get up and walk."

You might wonder, how did I know what to say? I sensed the gift of faith operating within me. I was convinced beyond a doubt that I was going to walk. I was convinced that the time was now.

I didn't realize, at the time, that I was prophesying. I was speaking to the audience about something that was about to take place. It was another "Watch and See" moment.

And then I began to shout, "ONE."

The patients were looking. I reached down to see if I could feel my thigh, but it was still numb. I just wanted to know if something had happened that I had gotten my feeling back, but it wasn't there.

Then I screamed, "TWO."

The patients were looking, and I was looking at them. I reached below my knees and I began to rub, but still I couldn't feel anything.

And then I shouted, "THREE."

The shout echoed in the atmosphere. The sound was ringing in my ears. The room was still.

When I shouted three, at the bottom of my heel I felt a burning sensation. I hadn't walked in almost five months. And now, I felt fire in the heel of my foot, in both of my feet. And it began to come up my legs and up my thighs and into my waist. This was a miracle. I reached forward and grabbed the parallel bars and with my legs on fire, I pulled myself forward. I realized that there was strength in my legs. The strength was there waiting for me to stand up.

I stood up for the first time. There was no one holding me. I wasn't using crutches or a walker. I wasn't pulling myself on a trapeze contraption or wheeling myself. I was standing, and I began to walk. I felt like my legs would break. It felt like I was walking on broken glass, but because I was blessed to feel an excruciating something in my legs, I was determined to keep going even with the sensation of needles. Because I had pain in my legs and feet, that I hadn't felt, I was blessed. I was glad to feel the pain. I realized what a blessing it was to feel and that if God didn't do anything else, I had regained the ability to feel even if it meant feeling pain. For the first time in my life, I'd considered the pain that I was feeling a good feeling!

Using the parallel bars, I turned, and walked back to the wheelchair.

The exhaustion from walking was consuming. I collapsed into the wheelchair. Sweat rolled down my face and dripped into my eyes. My back was sweat soaked.

The nurse yelled, "Let me get the doctor Mr. Johnson."

I turned to her and said, "I'm going to walk again."

WATCH and SEE

She began to shake as I proceeded to stand up and walk using the parallel bars. I turned around, but this time, I felt like I could've danced and rejoiced to celebrate my miracle.

I returned to my wheelchair in a state of shock, but I was exuberant with joy. Then I heard a patient, the wife of a world-renowned geneticist, began to scream at the top of her lungs.

"It's a miracle. Give me your faith."

She ran across the room at least 100 feet towards me. What should be noted is that this patient was in the hospital because she had a condition that did not allow her to step more than an inch at a time without excruciating pain. For her, walking was arduous and slow.

And yet, now, I saw her running towards me. She was screaming, "Give me your faith, give me your faith, give me your faith."

When she arrived at my chair, the Lord spoke to me and said, "Tell her to lay on your shoulders." This is something she would never have done before.

But she dropped her head on my shoulders. She began to weep, and I began to pray. I prayed aloud for salvation, forgiveness, deliverance, and healing for every person in the room.

The patient weeping on my shoulders began to scream, "Yes Lord, please God, please God."

The patients in physical therapy began to raise their hands in the air, some fell on their knees, and some walked the floor. Everyone prayed, even the nurse who wheeled me to the parallel bars. It was like we had been transported into a Pentecostal street revival, witnessing a great outpouring of God's power.

I had never witnessed this before outside of the four walls of the church or a formalized gathering of Christian believers. But in the hospital, in physical therapy, I witnessed the presence of God like never before. We were all swept up and raptured into the presence of God. His presence was so tangible until in that moment, I believe that there was no illness or condition that could not have been healed. Truly, this is the reason for miracles, to cause unbelievers to believe. Why else would God so demonstratively have orchestrated this time, at this moment? He could have healed me in my room, alone, with no onlookers. But the purpose of this divinely called encounter was to cause the other patients to believe.

Finally, I concluded the prayer and ended it with a shout of thanksgiving, I along with the patients and the nurse. I recall seeing most of the patients clapping and saying, "Hallelujah." They were crying. Some were praying. Others were hugging each other.

And then a doctor with a lab coat entered the room and walked directly to me.

He asked, "What is your name?"

I replied, "Marcus Johnson."

He asked, "Do you know what you just did?"

I said, "No sir, I don't."

He said, "You just healed my patient."

I said, "No sir I didn't."

He said, "Yes you did. I was at the door the entire time. I saw the whole thing. It is medically impossible for my patient to run. She has been in this hospital for six months. I have not been successful in getting her to mobilize and to move as she did today. You healed her."

I repeated, "No sir I did not. Her doctor healed her."

He responded, "But I am her doctor."

I replied, "No sir, you are a doctor, but Jesus Christ is The Doctor. He healed her."

That doctor shook his head. He walked over to his patient and began to converse with her.

The nurse announced that the physical therapy session for today was over!

She said, "You may now all return back to your rooms."

For the first time, while leaving physical therapy I could accompany my group, on foot, as we exited the therapy session. I used my wheelchair to guide my gait as I was walking, but I was aware that this regained activity was new and physically exerting.

We approached the big elevator knowing that everyone couldn't fit all at once. All the patients began to follow me to the elevator and were debating who would get on the elevator with me, as many as could fit got on the elevator together. We were so excited. We laughed, gasped for air, and talked. I insisted that I push my own wheelchair. I became very aware that even though I was walking, my balance was not steady. I used the wheelchair to steady myself, but it was evident that God and I were walking. We were walking together just as He promised.

Once on our floor, we entered the lobby from the elevator as a group. The nurses had to buzz the door to admit each of us onto the secured floor.

The patients announced to the nurses and other patients, "Look at this" as I was buzzed in and I entered beyond the glass, walking, and pushing my own wheelchair.

The nurses and other patients watched in amazement. A crowd followed me to my room asking me what had happened. The patients in the pain clinic wouldn't let me talk. They were telling my own story. I was excited but growing increasingly tired, so I asked if the crowd would leave so that I could sleep.

After a brief nap, I awakened. I lurched up to ensure that this was not a dream. Instantly, I could feel my legs; no more dead weight. I could still stand. I could still walk. For a while, whenever I would wake up, or I would want to walk, I would feel for my legs first. I needed the reassurance that I could still walk.

I got up and I began to wash my face. I could push the tray with the basin, placing my reacher to the side. Now, I could walk over to the sink. I splashed the water on my face and looked at myself in the mirror. I used the restroom because for months I relied on a bedpan. I was on a mission to do everything that had been done for me. Now, I wanted to do it myself.

Instead of eating in my room alone, I ate with the other patients in the dining hall. I had a Bible Study in my room that grew exponentially. We now met in the common area to accommodate the patients and the medical staff.

For many days, doctors entered my room, and I could see them gesturing and pointing at me. God had put me on display, and my miracle ultimately pointed all glory back to God.

Words of Wisdom to Readers

One of the hardest things in life is to believe God for the supernatural when there is no physical proof. When every report from experts, family, and friends appears contrary to a miracle, fear and doubt can and will set in.

However, when the appointed time for a turnaround comes, the entire audience, who is divinely invited, will be present. When everything that must occur first has preceded, from false reports, to facts, to human efforts, then the stage is set. It is here that God will often have us to prophesy according to His Word.

"And the Lord answered me, and said, Write the vision, and make it plain upon tables, that he may run that readeth it. For the vision is yet for an appointed time, but at the end it shall speak, and not lie: though it tarry, wait for it; because it will surely come, it will not tarry." Habakkuk 2:2-3 (KJV)

God knows how to activate the gift of faith. God knows how to motivate us lest we stagger at the promise. We must call those things that be not as though they already were. Our miracle, your miracle is guaranteed, but faith is the key ingredient.

Remember to not forget, God is waiting on the appointed time and the perfect moment.

The vision for my life, designed by God and prophesied by Mother Carrington, is depicted in the photographs that follow. The photographs were chosen to showcase significant moments throughout my journey as God revealed: His prophetic promise, the trial of my faith and the strength to endure, the fulfillment of His promise and the start of ministry, and ultimately, the beginning of my legacy. I also share these personal moments as visual representation that God has continued to keep His promises to me for decades. The photos are dated as evidence that God is faithful. "Watch and See."

MARCUS A. JOHNSON, SR.

Wedding photo - Marcus Sr. and Ronaé (June 1978)

Marcus Sr. directing the Mass Youth Choir at First United
Church of Jesus Christ Apostolic (July 1980)

WATCH and SEE

Marcus Sr. in his first return to church after his accident (March 1983)

Joseph Meyerhoff Symphony Hall - Marcus Sr. directs the Mass Youth choir (April 1983)

71

MARCUS A. JOHNSON, SR.

Marcus Sr. and Monaé at home (February 1984)

Marcus Sr., Ronaé, and Monaé (Summer 1984)

WATCH and SEE

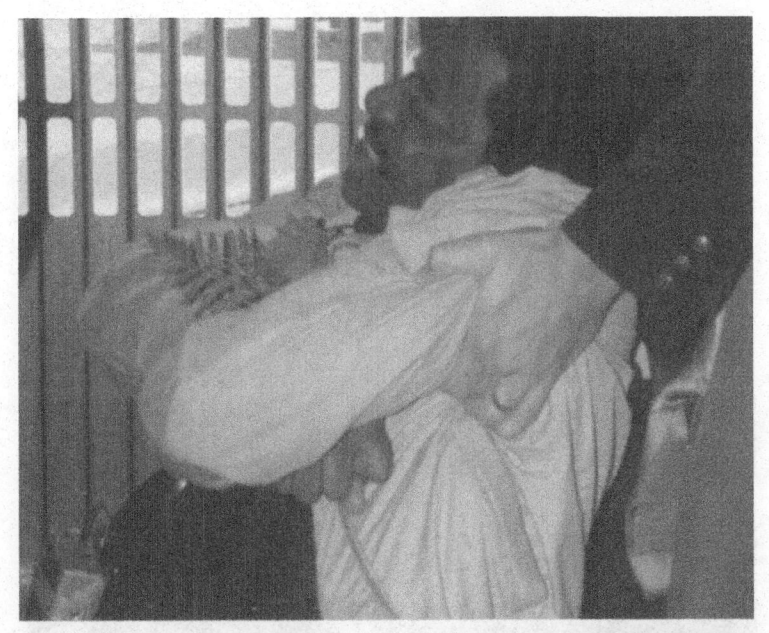

Marcus Sr. travels to Buffalo, NY for treatment (April 1986)

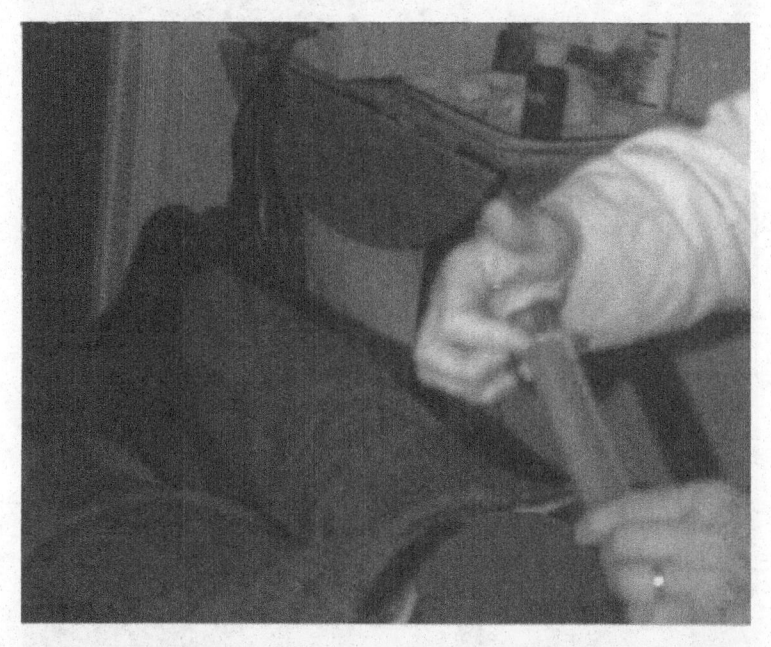

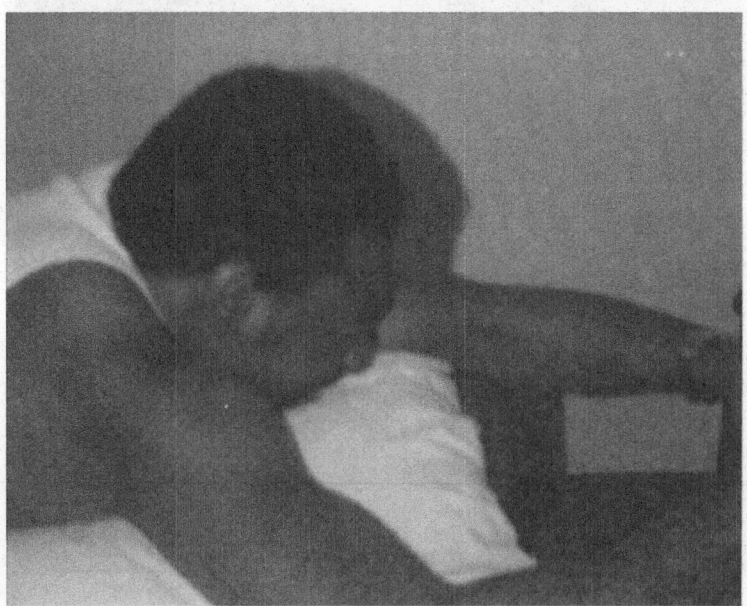

MARCUS A. JOHNSON, SR.

Marcus Sr. travels to Buffalo, NY for treatment (April 1986)

WATCH and SEE

The Pastoral Ordination of Marcus Sr. - The Late Chief Apostle Monroe Randolph Saunders, Sr., D.Min., Chief Officiant (December 2001)

The beginning days at New Harvest Ministries, Inc. (December 2001)

MARCUS A. JOHNSON, SR.

The 25th Wedding Celebration for Marcus Sr. and Ronaé – pictured with the Late Elijah Saunders, MD, FACC, FACP, FAHA, FASH (December 2003)

Elouise Johnson (Marcus Sr.'s mother), Ronaé, and Rosalee Banks (Ronaé's mother) (December 2003)

WATCH and SEE

The Johnson family on Easter Sunday - Monaé, Marcus Jr., Ronaé, and Marcus Sr. (March 2008)

Elouise and Mottomoes Johnson (Marcus Sr.'s parents) (March 2014)

MARCUS A. JOHNSON, SR.

As the father of the bride, moments before walking down the aisle - Monaé and Marcus Sr. (March 2014)

WATCH and SEE

The Raphael family - James, Little James, and Monaé (November 2016)

Dad's 60th Birthday Dinner - Marcus Sr. and Marcus Jr. (January 2017)

Chapter 11

FINDING THE NEW NORMAL

"And God is able to make all grace abound toward you; that ye, always having all sufficiency in all things, may abound to every good work:"
2 Corinthians 9:8 (KJV)

Many readers may feel that once a miracle has been performed and the Lord has answered prayers for victory, life becomes a smooth ride. Some may expect one sunny day after the next. And some look forward to calm breezy days on the beach. To be honest, I too had these same expectations. It seemed that my prayer request to walk again, pain free, with no dependency upon drugs, was my panacea. I expected that walking again would fix all my life's problems. But I was mistaken.

Please don't misunderstand my message. I am forever grateful to God for my miraculous healing. However, on the other side of my miracle, there were challenges that I and my immediate family confronted. Many of these challenges were irrelevant before I was healed. My new reality and norm came with a new set of issues and concerns.

For years, I have not understood how the sports industry handpicks talented youth, some of whom were raised in low-income households, and thrusts them into wealth and privilege overnight. The challenges of quick wealth, absent of the necessary safeguards such as legal and financial advisors, can lead to mismanagement of funds, gross debt, illegal activity, or vulnerability to charlatans attracted to their money and fame.

Well, in this same way, my miracle created a quick healing. Overnight I had new found abilities that were absent the day before. While my miracle remains priceless to me, it posed a new burden and stressors upon my family in several new ways.

MARCUS A. JOHNSON, SR.

For my wife, I required continuous care and support, on and off for about seven years. She learned to live with the trauma of a disabled husband. I was constantly at risk for falling, overdosing, and quite often needed to be monitored. She was accustomed to home care attendants, friends, and family staying with me to assist or watch out for my safety during the day while she went to work. Yet, with all this support, problematic circumstances still occurred. Crises still erupted: respiratory arrest, blood pressure spikes caused by pain, or erratic mood swings caused by depression, leading to irrational behaviors such as cooking late at night and falling asleep, and so many other poor choices.

My wife who had become my number one protector had to now adjust to her husband, seven years post-accident, who no longer needed around the clock protection and assistance. She had to learn how to be comfortable leaving me at home, alone, without fearing the worst would happen while she was at work, grocery shopping, or even just downstairs washing clothes. She had to learn that I could take a shower by myself. This might sound silly, but she describes the anxiety she felt releasing me to once again be independent. Even though we both prayed for this independence so fervently, now the time had come, but it became a new level of stress. The adjustment was all at once and overwhelming.

Often, we disagreed concerning whether I was able to drive alone or assume certain house chores that made her very anxious. Sometimes, she panicked that something negative was going to happen or that I was moving too fast for her comfort level. Yes, this was stressful.

Our parents also had to adjust. They were our first line of support, our backup support system. They were often the first ones we called when a crisis arose, or we needed additional hands in raising our daughter, help to do common chores around the house, or even just when I needed someone to sit with me, or to take me to a doctor's appointment. They, along with my siblings, and friends had adjusted their lives to accommodate our laundry list of needs. When I became healed, our parents struggled to let go and not fear that things would fall apart.

One episode that began the day after my miracle stands out in my mind. I knew in the depths of my heart that the Lord had delivered me instantly from the multiple prescription narcotics. Overtime, I had become addicted to taking these pills. Just like I started walking immediately, I instantly lost all cravings and desire to take the pills. I couldn't bear the thought of swallowing another narcotic. Yes, this was another a miracle.

When I signed myself out of the hospital because two psychotic patients on my ward were jealous of my miracle and threatened to physically assault me, my wife, our daughter, and I temporarily went to my parents' house so we could have backup help, and just for safety precautions while my wife went to work.

WATCH and SEE

It was there that I announced to my wife and parents that I was no longer planning to take any more prescription drugs. It was like I had detonated an emotional bomb.

One may ask, "What's the problem with that?"

Well, this was a huge problem. The doctors at Hospital D had strongly discouraged me from leaving the hospital suddenly. They insisted that I was at high risk of relapsing, despite my miracle. More critically, they pressed that I needed to be monitored if I were to be weaned off the many high dosages of narcotics. They further stated that my wife and mother would be responsible for my relapse, extreme withdrawals, and possible death since I signed myself out of the hospital against their recommendation. Their policy protecting all patients' rights, forbid them from separating any patients from each other. Certainly, no separation could be enforced since I was "merely threatened" (their words, not mine). I was not willing to chance being attacked and physically assaulted. Therefore, my wife and mother assisted me in leaving the hospital. We were all warned repeatedly of my impending relapse, but we left anyway.

Needless to say, my wife and parents were in a frenzy. They didn't know what to do. On one hand, they saw the miraculous answer from God to their prayers for my healing. On the other hand, they were unsure about my timing for leaving, knowing I could not stay at the hospital unprotected for my safety. Then my refusal to take the prescribed narcotics left the entire house in a tizzy.

Both my wife and parents tried to convince me to stay on the medications until a doctor would give a careful and regimented weaning process. Yet, in my spirit I knew the Lord had completely delivered me. I had no doubt about this. However, sensing my wife and parents' anxiety and frustration over this new miracle, I compromised and agreed to take one more dosage of my narcotics. I agreed to this only the first night after leaving the hospital. I agreed only for their sake. I told each of them that after that night, I was not taking any more of those drugs.

I remember my wife and mom, respectively, coming in the bedroom trying to change my mind about stopping the drugs cold turkey. I knew I was frustrating and scaring them, but I also knew the Lord was doing a new thing in my life, and I wanted Him to complete His work.

Now, let me make myself clear. I would never ever encourage anyone to disobey or disregard their doctor's instructions. Under normal circumstances, this is ill-advised. However, a miracle changes everything. A miracle interrupts protocol. The woman with the issue of blood crawled through the crowd to touch Jesus' garment (Luke 8:43-48 KJV). The centurion's servant was healed when Jesus spoke the word (Matthew 8:5-13 KJV). Great faith produces a great miracle. A great miracle interrupts the norm.

MARCUS A. JOHNSON, SR.

My circumstances had been interrupted by a great miracle. God was still unfolding my miracle and testimony. Just as He directed me through the tunnel from the crystal clear water and green pasture outside of the City called Heaven; just as He spoke to me in the ceiling of Hospital A as my spirit suspended over my lifeless body and the medical team fervently worked to revive me; just as the Lord said to me "Watch and See" I knew He had delivered me from those narcotics. Just as confidently as He enabled me to rise from my wheelchair and begin walking after almost five months of paralysis, I knew I was instantly detoxed by the Holy Ghost. I repudiated the thought of drug dependency.

Again, this was not wishful or positive thinking, but a definite spiritual witness within me. I knew God had delivered me. That is the only reason I was so adamant not to give into my loved one's request. Even after they contacted my pastor and family physician, who in earnest out of a sincere love for me tried to convince me to continue the medications, I knew in my heart that I was delivered completely. They even urged me to consider returning to the pain clinic program at the hospital as an inpatient. But, I held my ground as I explained my conviction, yet I appreciated and valued their sincerest concern for me. God wasn't dealing with them as He was dealing with me. I had to understand and be confident in this.

Meanwhile, the hospital continued to call my parents house, where I was staying, threatening my wife and parents that they would be complicit and culpable in my demise. They predicted that I would have imminent convulsions and traumatic withdrawal rendering me violent and psychotic. My family had to listen to the medical experts scientifically predict the risk of my fatal outcome, while listening to my conviction and determination that God had healed me.

Yes, there was a lot of stress and trauma during my post-miracle. Remember, all stress is not negative, but it still feels heavy and trying. The scripture comes to mind, "For unto whomsoever much is given, of him shall be much required: and to whom men have committed much, of him they will ask the more." Luke 12:48 (KJV)

God had delivered me for certain. For the record, I never experienced any convulsions, violent or psychotic reactions, withdrawal symptoms, or any of the horrible scenarios the physicians predicted. I believe that God used every moment of these long days, where I knew everyone was just waiting and watching, to grow my faith and our confidence in Him.

Ultimately, with all my confidence in God and an obvious operation of the gift of faith, I felt like a modern-day Elijah. Remember, Elijah called down fire from Heaven on Mt. Carmel to demonstrate that His God was the true God. After He destroyed the false prophets, Jezebel threatened him. Elijah, the great prophet, ran out of fear and hid under a juniper tree having a pity party. 1 Kings 19:1-5 (KJV)

As the Lord had to deal with Elijah, He had to deal with me. After convincing my wife, family, church, and friends that I would be fine and for them to allow me to walk out my miracle through independence, I would then experience momentary bouts of fear. Why? Simply stated, I'm also very human. And humanity is full of frailties.

I can remember, waking up during the night or in the morning panicked that I only had been dreaming about my miracle. I was afraid that I was still paralyzed. This was often a secret storm that I chose not to share to avoid creating fear in others. I also remember having unsuspected panic attacks when I would step outside of my house feeling the big outdoors would swallow me up. I had spent so much time inside hospital rooms for such long stays that I was afraid to leave my house. Going outside, even for just a walk, was too much. I was afraid. Again, I tried to camouflage my emotions from my family and sometimes I was unsuccessful as they could detect my change of emotions.

Finally, I had to tackle my fear of applying for employment after seven years of being on disability. I had learned to receive so much bad news and disappointments throughout the seven years from the doctor telling me after my surgery that I would be out of work for at least six months. Then one major surgery became two, then three, with so many complications. Four major surgeries became nine. After surviving all of that, I had to confront the giant fear of rejection. When I applied for jobs, I was often denied because I had been out of the labor market for over seven years. I was healed, but employers believed I was a high risk and therefore labeled me unemployable. Every interviewer wanted to know what have you been doing for the past eight years? When I told them of my accident, they feared their potential liability in hiring a prior disabled employee, originally injured on the job, and who filed a claim.

After several, "don't call us, we'll call you" and "sorry you're not exactly what we're looking for," I began to realize that I didn't go through this journey to remain unemployed. I realized that with every test comes a testimony. God had given me a testimony and it would usher me into my destined opportunities. After about six months, I began to land jobs, opportunities, and I found my place in ministry.

Words of Wisdom to Readers

Yes, very few discuss the stressors and burdens that occur after a miracle or blessing. Many people focus upon the trauma before the crisis and the miraculous deliverance. But God does a complete work. We must be co-laborers with Christ as we share the weight throughout the entire process. God will teach perseverance and faithfulness in the process.

Moreover, the same faithful God that keeps us until the miracle, is the same God that performs the miracle, and is the same God that will sustain

the miracle. Regardless of obstacles and challenges, God can finish whatever He has started even until the end.

According to the Apostle Paul, "Being confident of this very thing, that he which hath begun a good work in you will perform it until the day of Jesus Christ." Philippians 1:6 (KJV)

After He gives us a miracle, we are tasked to carry the miracle in the form of our testimony and witness wherever we go. Every day will not be met with a unanimous audience urging us to go ahead. Sometimes, we will meet well intentioned opponents or reserved persons who may not share our conviction at our same level. Every day will not be sunny, breezy, and calm on the beach. However, our miracle must become personal as our faith is personal. Regardless of who believes or doubts, we must remain "...steadfast, unmoveable, always abounding in the work of the Lord, forasmuch as ye know that your labour is not in vain in the Lord." 1 Corinthians 15:58 (KJV)

A major fear that some people who are healed may feel is that the miracle may be temporary. Yet, the Word of God addresses this fear as torment. "Now unto him that is able to keep you from falling, and to present you faultless before the presence of his glory with exceeding joy." Jude 1:24 (KJV)

In other words, any miracle that God gives is secure. He alone prevents us from returning to the pre-miracle conditions. God will catapult us into our destiny with great joy and fulfillment. If we relapse for any reason, remember though we may fall, we can always get back up again. "For a just man falleth seven times, and riseth up again..." Proverbs 24:16a (KJV)

Ultimately, the healed are added to the great cloud of witnesses that will instruct, guide, and encourage others. Just as many young athletes are ushered into great wealth after signing a contract and need mentorship and accountability advisors, we can become spiritual mentors and accountability advisors to others, post-miracle.

Chapter 12

MY MIRACLE SON

> *"And the floors shall be full of wheat, and the vats shall overflow with wine and oil. And I will restore to you the years that the locust hath eaten, the cankerworm, and the caterpillar, and the palmerworm, my great army which I sent among you. And ye shall eat in plenty, and be satisfied, and praise the name of the Lord your God, that hath dealt wondrously with you: and my people shall never be ashamed."*
> *Joel 2:24-26 (KJV)*

Looking back to 1983, I can see that God had miraculously helped my brother and sister-in-law to survive the death of her father. They funeralized and buried him within days of their wedding. That was a miracle indeed. Many souls were saved at the Homegoing Service. This too was another miracle.

On the night of February 22, 1983, when the sheetrock fell on me, I was physically dead and crossed over through the tunnel of light to the other side. I heard the Lord call my name and tell me to go back and declare that Heaven is a real place—that was also a miracle.

Then with the loss of my job and our income being cut to less than half of what we were used to, as I waited for my worker's compensation benefits to begin, the Lord still allowed my wife and me during this time to purchase our first home. After being turned down for the loan, we prayed, and the Federal Housing Administration (FHA) rescinded their first decision. Upon reconsideration, they backed our loan—and that was a miracle.

Thinking about my second surgery when a pulmonary embolism (blood clot in my lungs), traveled from my leg to my lungs, and I was pronounced dead in Hospital A only to return to the other side and hear the Lord tell me to go back and to declare that Heaven is a real place—another miracle.

God granted me the privilege to lie on the bed and to open my eyes and begin to praise Him and glorify Him after the doctor had pronounced me dead. I could share with the medical doctors and the attending nurses what I saw from the ceiling as they watched my dead body. Days later, in that same bed, I began to tell them precise details about what I had seen in the room throughout all of the chaotic activity, but as a surviving living witness. That was a miracle.

And then, living through all the traumatic incidents, excessive amounts of prescription drugs, 100 pills a day, blood pressure 270 over 230 and God spared me from a stroke and a heart attack, just another miracle.

Having to go through all the anxiety of bills being paid and waiting for income and yet God allowed the electricity to stay on and for food to be on the table. It was a miracle.

God granted me the dignity to still be a father to my daughter and a husband to my wife. It was a miracle. At intervals within the seven years I would experience a level of recovery, go back to my church, direct a 200-voice youth choir, and lead them in worship through song. Even though I would relapse, I would come back again, over, and over and over teaching the choir the hymns of the church and the songs of worship that became more real to me throughout this faith journey. I testified of the goodness of the Lord, even when it didn't look like it was working for me, even when I didn't feel like it was working for me. Yet, I maintained that personal encounter with God, not because I'm perfect but because it was all that I had. This was my miracle.

After being admitted into Hospital B where an older male patient wandered into my room, as sick as I was, where God granted me the opportunity to minister to him the plan of salvation, only to discover an hour later, that the nurses were looking for him. He had wandered away from his room after first disconnecting himself from his IVs. They returned him to his room and less than a couple of hours later, he died. God sent him my way first, so that I could share the gospel of Jesus Christ and know that one day, I will see him again. That was a miracle.

Even after the boiler room explosion in Hospital C where I was spared as an inpatient, God enabled me less than two months later, after my sixth surgery, to drive my car. While in route to a doctor's visit, there was a car that ran a stop sign and struck me sideways. My car spun around in the street and was turned on its side. Even though I had to be cut out of the car by the fire department, God, in all his grace and his power, did not let the car explode. The Lord protected me in all of that. Even though the street was blocked off by the police as the firemen were cutting me out of the car, a woman appeared with a baby in her arms calling my full name. She said that God had sent her there to tell me that everything was going to be alright. As I gazed at the baby in her arms, I realized that the baby was a great symbol, representing me in the arms of God. She vanished. Both the firemen and I were shocked that she appeared that close to the car and that she

WATCH and SEE

was now gone. How could this be? Was she an angel in the flesh? Most certainly she was. I'm so grateful that the firemen and police also saw her, so I wouldn't doubt. Just another miracle.

Over seven years, of just one miracle after another, after another and, now, I could walk again—another miracle.

The greatest miracle to culminate it all was still to be seen. In 1988, two doctors at Hospital B told me that it was doubtful that I would have another child. They explained that due to the extensive effects of my illness, numerous surgeries, and medications, it was uncertain that I would be able to father more children. I can hear them speaking now, "be grateful that you have a daughter."

But on January 7, 1990, just two days after my 33rd birthday, the Lord blessed my wife and me to have a son: Marcus Aaron Johnson, Jr. He was born on a Sunday morning.

The miracles don't stop. They continue, but my son is the extension of the miracles and proof that what God promised, God will perform.

In the late 1970s, Mother Carrington prophesied that my wife and my children would stand with me in ministry. I didn't know what that prophetic word meant. I couldn't fully comprehend it then, and I like Mary, simply pondered this in my heart. Even when I thought I knew, I still didn't fully know what it meant. There were so many scenes in between the promise and the fulfillment of promise, and I just didn't have a clue. Yet, God knew and therefore sent a word out of time (out of season) to keep me throughout seven years in every season of hardship.

And now Marcus, Jr., is a man. He's my miracle son.

He excelled in his formative and secondary education and became a scholar at the University of Maryland College Park. In 2011, he began his graduate studies at Princeton University with a passion for Immigration and Latin American Studies. He has travelled to Spain, Mexico, Panama, and Sweden pursuing academic and field research and attending professional conferences. Today, as a U.S. Fulbright Research Grant Fellow, Marcus graduated with his PhD in Politics and Social Policy from Princeton University in June 2017. I cannot put into words how proud I am of my son and namesake.

It is so ironic that when he was a young child, I often wondered if my years of medication really affected him because he was very hyperactive. God knows I struggled to keep him calm and still.

Interestingly, my daughter was so obedient and just easy to take care of. I barely reprimanded her, and she would just easily comply. But not my son. He came out of my wife's stomach screaming, and he screamed through his infancy, and he bounced as a toddler. Somewhere during elementary school, he became conscientious and showed a soft heart. He gave his heart to the Lord at a very young age. He always cared for others who were mistreated, sticking up for them as though he were their valiant protector.

When I think that he developed a passion on his own to become fluent in Spanish and to study abroad, I can only wonder, "but who could know the mind of God." Marcus has been integral in translating my sermons for Spanish speaking visitors that have come to the church. My missions' trips to Uruguay and repeatedly to Cuba, forged with my covenant brother Bishop Angel Nuñez, are somehow all connected to my son of promise. Marcus and I share a passion for helping people—in particular, the vulnerable, under-represented, overlooked, and often marginalized persons. Only God could imprint the same passion for serving the underserved deep inside both of us.

Thanks be unto God for being the true promise keeper and for continuing to complete the work in me that He began. For what remains, I continue to trust him to work out that work in me which He has already established.

Words of Wisdom to Readers

"The thief cometh not, but for to steal, and to kill, and to destroy: I am come that they might have life, and that they might have it more abundantly." John 10:10 (KJV)

It is important to note that God will send a promise before its fulfillment. The promise might be vague or the promise might be clear. However, in as much as we think that we understand it, in time we will learn that the promise is always bigger, greater, more expansive, and ever increasing. It is always so much more than we understood. As we walk out our journey by faith, the promise will grow as we allow God to enlarge himself within us.

Understand that Satan's strategy is to steal our dream to kill our purpose so that he can destroy our potential. If he can accomplish this strategy, he will delay or intercept the fulfillment of God's promise in our lives. Note, he can only accomplish this with our cooperation. Satan cannot take anything away from us except God allows it for a season. We must either hand it over or allow him full reign in our territory. However, we should understand that God gives the promise so we can hold onto the hand of the promise keeper. He must remain the object of our faith, our praise, our prayer, and our worship. In so doing, we will overcome the strategy of Satan. Clearly, Satan has come to keep us from our expected end. But Jesus promised that He came to give us life and that more abundantly. His purpose from the very beginning is to restore to us everything that mankind has handed over to the enemy or what we allowed him to steal by ransacking our territory.

Satan thought that he could destroy my potential by robbing me of my dream. The accident and multiple surgeries almost accomplished that. The more I listened to the doctors and viewed my circumstances, the more I became challenged in believing God for my fulfillment. When I would hit my rock bottoms and go as low as I could go, there was nowhere to look but up into the face of God, my promise keeper. He constantly reminded me, "For I know the thoughts that I think toward you...thoughts of peace and not of evil, to give you a future..." Jeremiah 29:11(NKJV)

He is the restorer of those things that have been lost. Whatever your challenges may be, remember that for every believer in Jesus Christ, God has made a promise. Don't allow any obstacles to cause you to give up on your blessed destiny. Hold on to God and things will turn. The miracle is always in what remains.

"And let us not be weary in well doing: for in due season we shall reap, if we faint not." Galatians 6:9 (KJV)

Chapter 13

THERE IS LAUGHTER IN MY PAIN

*"A merry heart doeth good like a medicine: but
a broken spirit drieth the bones."
Proverbs 17:22 (KJV)*

Most times when I refer to my testimony—being crushed by 2,400 lbs of sheetrock, recovering from nine major surgeries, living with extremely elevated blood pressure, being addicted to 100 prescription drugs daily, experiencing severe insomnia, managing chronic pain and the list goes on—the tone is quite serious. However, despite these somber realities, there were also pleasant moments and events that lifted my spirits. These times often stopped emotional downward spirals and temporarily turned my shadows and dark clouds into smiles and laughter.

I would like to recount a few of these moments as they taught me that laughter is literally like medicine to our souls. Because I was so reliant on medication, I can honestly say that laughter often alleviated the pain in my heart. It helped me to shift my focus from the obvious challenges and hardships I faced. It caused me not to miss the many subtle joys and sublime pleasures that were hidden in such challenging experiences. If we let them, pleasantries can teach us vital life lessons and give us comfort so we can accept the wisdom of God's plan.

First, there were many smiles concerning our young daughter Monaé, who was only two years old at the time of my accident. Once when I was rushed to the hospital in an ambulance, a nightmarish event that unfortunately happened often, the paramedics arrived to treat my violent spasmodic episode.

My parents and siblings came to our home to accompany my wife and daughter to the hospital. While they sat in the waiting room awaiting the doctor's diagnosis, my mom asked Monaé, who was about four years old to take off her coat. Everyone was settling in for a long wait and was getting more comfortable.

I'm told Monaé, who was preoccupied while playing with her dolls, suddenly stopped playing and developed a very sad countenance. She then responded to my Mom, "I can't." For those of us who knew Monaé as a child, we remember how gentle, respectful, and obedient she was. This response was very much out of character and strange. She certainly would not refuse her grandmother's instruction.

My mother asked, "Why can't you take off your coat?"

Monaé then looked at her uncles and grandfather and insisted, "I can't!"

My mom proceeded to open her coat and suddenly broke into a smile. My mom realized that in everyone's haste to leave the house for the hospital no one noticed that Monaé had put on her coat right over her underwear and slip. She didn't have on any clothes. She was too embarrassed to be exposed before everyone in the waiting room.

My mom laughed and permissioned Monaé to keep wearing her coat. My family tells me that a roaring laughter broke through the tension and stress in the waiting room. The painful emotions were converted into a temporary release. My family found relief in this humor, the medicine that was needed in that moment.

Certainly, unforgettable smiles and laughter kept my wife and me through years of financial struggles. For many years, our household income was drastically reduced because I lost my full-time salary, and we were dependent upon my worker's compensation along with my wife's income.

Whereas we were used to more extravagant celebrations, birthdays, holidays, and anniversaries, our lives became quite different as we had to re-prioritize our expenditures.

Well thank God for our family because they came through for us supplementing our lack, especially for Monaé's birthdays, school programs, pictures, pageants, and holidays.

This one year my wife and I were celebrating our milestone tenth wedding anniversary. Yet, we had no extra money to dine out at a restaurant, not to mention the extra expense for my special transportation needs and babysitting cost. My wife had become the primary bread winner, and I did not want to add anymore burden upon her plate.

Consequently, we brainstormed a creative idea. How could we have a going out to dinner experience but catered in our own home for free? Well, my wife is an excellent cook, and she prepared a scrumptious anniversary meal. We designed special menus with prices. Then we got dressed up and stepped outside. After waiting a few moments, we rang our own doorbell, and my wife's sisters opened our front door. They were both dressed as formal waitresses and welcomed us into a decorated make-shift restaurant. Everything from the table cloth, china, flatware, centerpieces, and aprons were all ours, but it seemed like we were at a restaurant.

My lovely sisters-in-law served us as professionally trained waitresses. Their service created more merriment as we were all acting out our designed anniversary drama. My wife and I pretended to be wealthy celebrities as we exchanged personally crafted cards and make-pretend gifts.

I do believe this was one of the most enjoyable anniversaries we have had since being married in 1978. Yes, since that tenth anniversary, we have traveled abroad, stayed in resorts, eaten in top tier restaurants, and ridden chauffeured in limousines, but none can compare with the thrill and joy of this inexpensive anniversary. This night brought us so much joy and laughter for many days afterwards. We continued to savor the great fulfillment and fun, despite my physical pain. We disallowed all woes and regrets for just one evening we would never forget. And it was all worth it!

Words of Wisdom to Readers

Whenever, God starts blessing, Satan starts tampering with the blessing. When we receive a blessing or a miracle from God, we must guard it as a treasure. Why? The enemy knows that a miracle is birthed out of great trials and becomes our testimony purchased by Jesus' Blood. "And they overcome him (Satan) by the Blood of the Lamb, and by the Word of their testimony; and they loved not their lives unto death." Revelation 12:11 (KJV)

No matter how hopeless things appear, there is the joy of the Lord waiting to be released. "...in everything give thanks for this is the will of God in Christ Jesus concerning you." 1 Thessalonians 5:18 (KJV)

God gives us a good sense of humor, because there is laughter even in our pain!

Chapter 14

COME OVER TO THIS SIDE OF JORDAN

> *"For I know the thoughts that I think toward you, saith the Lord, thoughts of peace, and not of evil, to give you an expected end."*
> Jeremiah 29:11 (KJV)

In retrospect, as I look back over the path that God chartered for my "Watch and See" journey, I can see that it was at times an uphill-climb, then a downward-slope, yet it was filled with many plateaus. I can presently appreciate the journey even though I didn't know that leaving Egypt, where everything was familiar to me, would entail crossing my Red Sea of sickness with years of wandering in the wilderness. At the end of the wilderness, I crossed the Jordan River and walked on dry ground into the Promised Land. To this day, thirty-four years after the sheetrock fell upon me, I am still conquering challenges which present themselves. No matter who you are, challenges will come.

The reality remains that if I had known any of the challenges that lay ahead of me, I would have run the other way or attempted to avoid all the chaos and drama for fear it would be overwhelming and too much to bear. God couldn't tell me ahead of time about my sister-in-law (and brother) losing their father three days before the wedding; or that his funeral would occur two days after the wedding; or that I would enter the stock room at Kinney's Shoe Store where 2,400 lbs of sheetrock would fall, crushing my body; or that the accident would cause me to die and usher me into my first out-of-body experience; or that I would have nine major surgeries; or that a second out-of-body-experience would occur; or that I would experience numerous ambulance transports to the hospital; or that chronic pain and paralysis would lead to drug addiction to prescription pills; or that I would battle financial hardships and depression and heartache. If He told me that I would endure an uphill-climb, then a downward-slope, and many plateaus for seven years, I wouldn't have survived the incomprehensible shock. For like you, I would have counted the seconds, hours, days, weeks, months, and years as I laid on my back unable to walk. I would have been consumed in desperation, and my faith would have been extinguished.

But God in His infinite wisdom and perfect plan tried me in the fire and produced a testimony of pure gold. The Lord knew that I as a little boy tapped into His heartbeat as I desired a great testimony. I couldn't articulate what I felt in words, but I wanted to be a living witness proclaiming the continued power of God from a firsthand experience.

I recall from the age of six to twelve how I would take my Lincoln Log cabin sets and build churches and sanctuaries in my bedroom. They were filled with make believe people who I pretended were worshipping and praising God. Then a relative, no different from siblings through play today, would knock my church structures down just to provoke my emotional response of anger. I fought him back in retribution and vengeance.

Yet, despite all of the many churches that were knocked down, I became more determined to rebuild them larger and stronger. Unintentionally, unknowingly, there was a pastor in the making inside of me who was determined to withstand opposition and restore brokenness and to minister the gospel of Jesus Christ to hurting people. Though many are broken, sick, and destitute, they cannot be left this way. Someone must minister to them and "...preach good tidings unto the meek...bind up the brokenhearted...proclaim liberty to the captives, and the opening of the prison to them that are bound." Isaiah 61:1 (KJV)

I believe God used my entire life to prepare me to be "...steadfast, unmoveable, always abounding in the work of the Lord..." 1 Corinthians 15:58 (KJV) Though my physical body, soul, and spirit were ultimately knocked down, and I suffered broken limbs, seemingly insurmountable odds, dysfunction through many hospital stays, serious surgeries, numerous physical and psychological therapies, many prayers would seem to go unanswered on my behalf, but God had a plan. The Lord was faithful to restore me throughout the many setbacks and falls that occurred repeatedly.

Had I not taken this journey, I believe I would have never shared the gospel with so many souls across this country and throughout the world in Mexico, Cuba, Israel, Uruguay, the Caribbean, Africa, South Africa, Europe, Canada, and the U.S. proclaiming the miraculous power of God that is still available today.

I'm sure New Harvest Ministries, Inc., that the Lord graced me to found and pastor, may never have been birthed just a few blocks away from the hospital where I was miraculously healed from paralysis. In 1999 when the church was founded, the neighborhood was blighted with abandoned and boarded houses, streets full of rival gangs, and a heavy prevalence of drug dealing and addiction. This ministry seemed like an impossible setup. However, the Lord challenged me to lead the New Harvest congregation to "Watch and See" Him transform us and the community where we minister. God had a master plan. Through the wisdom of late Chief Apostle Monroe R. Saunders, Sr., D.Min., God sent me to southeast Baltimore City to build a work for Him. To minister to the meek, brokenhearted, captive, and the bound population. What I have come to really understand is that people get knocked down by the heavy weights of life. Hardships, disappointments, and abuses break them. Everyone doesn't have a loving family and friends to pray for them, to love them, to encourage them, and sometimes to even carry them through life's difficulties. For these reasons and many others, people are addicted to drugs, substances, vices, harmful relationships, and other poisons.

Here in southeast Baltimore, just blocks away from where God healed me, I am preaching in the sanctuary, much different from the Lincoln Log structures I built as a child, filled with people singing and praising God. I've ministered in this community and on the streets to many persons. This is what I've learned; people all over the world (from South Africa to Baltimore) are hungry for the good news of Jesus Christ. People are looking for hope and truth.

I know, firsthand, that there are no words of gloom and doom powerful enough to pronounce death, hopelessness, meaninglessness, purposelessness, or paralysis which God cannot override. I am a living witness that God is able. He is fully aware of the impossibilities with man. He is aware of all the incredible barriers and multiple defeats. He knows of every attempt to self-medicate to numb the radiating emotional pain that comes from crushing news and heartaches. He knows that disappointments can weary the soul.

God is not making light of these conditions, but He is saying "Watch and See."

Watch all the obstacles that echo defeat.

Watch for the naysayers and even well intentioned realists who suggest that one simply roll-over and accept a negative plight. Give up the ghost and die.

Instead, we should watch. Observe every detail that seems to suggest we will not survive the wilderness. Instead, we should see. Trust God, the true miracle worker who heals and delivers.

We must "Watch and See" the Red Sea block our future, until God moves.

We must stand still when we have done everything to believe God and See the salvation of the Lord in our situations.

We must See God open the Red Sea as He invites us to arise out of our despair and cross over the very blockages and barriers that stand in our way.

I proclaim that as He showed up in the Old Testament for the patriarchs, as He showed up in the New Testament for the Apostles, as He showed up in centuries past making new ways that did not pre-exist, as He showed up in my complex circumstances where expert physicians had exhausted their best expertise with no breakthroughs on my behalf, as He showed up for me in the hospital and manifested my miraculous healing, I believe He will continue to do this for you.

Try Him! I invite you to "Watch and See" God bring you across your Jordan River into your Promised Land of destiny and divine purpose in the earth. He will give you a testimony of true victory in the very same places where you once stood defeated and left alone. Wherever you have been knocked down, have fallen, or are about to fall, God is able and willing to raise you up. He will give you a testimony that will bring Him glory as it ministers to others. It's not over. "Watch and See!"

Let me take this time to offer two prayers for any reader who has not accepted the Lord Jesus as Savior, or who desires to recommit to Christ. Dear reader, you too can experience your miracle of rebirth. I invite you to pray either of these prayers along with me.

First, let's pray a prayer for salvation.

"Dear Jesus, I do believe You are the miracle worker that can raise the dead. I know that without You I am spiritually dead and lost. Yet, I do believe according to the Scriptures that You died on the cross to pay the price for my sins. I do believe You were buried to take all of my sins away. I do believe God the Father raised You from the grave. Today, I place my faith in You. I invite You into my life as my Savior and Lord. I receive You by faith as God's gift of grace. I believe that one day I will have eternal life in Heaven. Thank You for saving me right now. In Jesus Name I pray. Amen."

Second, let's pray a prayer for recommitment to God.

"Dear Jesus, I have received salvation and am born again, but over time I have wandered away. Like the prodigal son who left his father's house for the far country, I have prioritized other things. My priorities have replaced my relationship with You. Forgive me Lord for forgetting my first love. Refill me with Your Spirit that I may live my life close to thee. I recommit my heart to You. Thank You for meeting me right where I am. Thank You for accepting me because You have never stopped loving me. In Jesus Name I pray. Amen."

Whichever prayer you prayed, thank God for His mercy and grace.

You are prepared to cross your Jordan. I believe that you too will "Watch and See" a miraculous move of God.

Words of Wisdom to Readers

"Behold, I am the Lord, the God of all flesh: is there any thing too hard for me?" Jeremiah 32:27 (KJV)

Crossing Jordan is the major passageway out of the wilderness and signifies the exit from an Egyptian captivity. It leads from wandering in the wilderness to inheriting the promise of God to fulfill destiny in the earth. Often, after many milestones have been accomplished, the devil will pose a

WATCH and SEE

challenge that appears insurmountable. The purpose of this challenge is to cause the intended recipient of the promise to forfeit destiny.

Yet, God foreknows and foresees every trial. He alone can preapprove a trial to validate His work in us. Whereas Egypt couldn't kill us, the Red Sea could not drown us, and the wilderness could not block us, now the Jordan River must become a passageway to our promised land. It cannot block us from the intended purpose for which we were born.

As the old gospel song says, "I don't believe He brought me this far to leave me." Remember, what God has started He will finish. In tough times, square your shoulders, rehearse the Word of God in your heart, and walk in the steps that God has already ordered for your life. Take faith and courage. Cross the Jordan. God will send all the help you need.

"Watch and See."

Epilogue

I'M COMMITTED TO FINISH THE WORK

"Now unto him that is able to do exceeding abundantly above all that we ask or think, according to the power that worketh in us."
Ephesians 3:20 (KJV)

Watch and See documents more than five decades of evidence that God often does His best work under our worst circumstances. He allows conditions to become the most unfavorable as we watch the sand in the hour glass run out. He allows us to exhaust resources and our best efforts until we are left to depend upon only God. It's in that moment that we come to an unshakeable, irrefutable, and undeniable revelation that God is faithful. God really is our all and all.

After years of watching God work in my life, I've seen doors open for me that would have never existed with great audiences and small groups. I've walked into opportunities that would have never been extended with renown political leaders as well as gang members. I've ministered in prisons and on street corners. I've traveled across these United States and internationally to minister God's Word and to share my testimony with the saved and unsaved. In addition, God has given me a special empathy for the sick and the dying. I continuously serve in hospitals and at the point of crisis. In these moments, people (saved and unsaved) need to feel the comforting love of God. Therefore, I am compelled to testify and encourage others to overcome their challenges and to blossom in places of captivity, following the example of Daniel, Shadrach, Meshach, and Abednego. Daniel 3:18 (KJV)

Most recently in South Africa, I had the great pleasure to meet Archbishop Desmond Tutu. In just a few moments, I shared with him portions of *Watch and See*.

Much work still lies ahead for me and like Paul I will continue until I can say, "the time of my departure is at hand. I have fought a good fight, I have finished my course, I have kept the faith: Henceforth there is laid up for me a crown of righteousness, which the Lord, the righteous judge, shall give me at that day: and not to me only, but unto all them also that love his appearing." 2 Timothy 4:6-8 (KJV)

I often reflect back to my conversation with God in 1983. In my second out of body experience, I stood at the threshold of eternity and time and made a promise to God (my heavenly Father). I committed to return to earth and live out the rest of my life finishing the work that He created me to do. I do not believe that purpose is arbitrary. It is given by God, orchestrated, and deliberate. Nearly twenty-five years later, on August 8, 2008, I stood at my spiritual father's bedside, the Late Chief Apostle Monroe Randolph Saunders, Sr., D.Min. Nearly an hour before he transitioned from this life into his blessed eternal home, I promised him (my spiritual father) that I would finish the work that he had ordained me to do.

Now, almost ten years later, I continue to fulfill these mandates. For me time is of the essence. I am bound by an eternal oath to live out my purpose, to fulfill my destiny, and to develop every facet of the ministry that God has given me. I will write many more books, teach many more lessons, and preach many more sermons. I will produce plays and use a variety of formats to share my testimony. I prayed at the age of twelve for a testimony and God granted my request. Therefore, I must continue to testify and tell everyone that Heaven is a real place.

God has numbered each of our days, and I don't know how much time remains for me. But when I meet God again, I want to hear "Well done." I want to be able to say I HAVE FINISHED THE WORK. Like Paul, I want to be able to say I HAVE FINISHED MY COURSE.

My dear reader, there is a divine purpose for every step and misstep in your journey.

"Watch and See!"

Acknowledgments

My first acknowledgment is to my Creator, Father, and Healer. I thank You for keeping me and letting me live. I thank You for giving me a testimony. I thank You for entrusting me as a witness to tell everyone of Your magnificent power and glory. God, because of You I am.

I want to acknowledge my parents who raised me in a Christian home full of love and security, and my two late grandmothers, Dear and Lorraine, who are both in a class all their own. Collectively, your continued prayers and hands on support throughout this journey has enabled me to write this work.

To each of my siblings (Nathan, Sam, David, Chelly, and Stevie), I cannot put my love for you or our group text messages into words. The best is still yet to come.

To my in-laws, Rosalee Banks and the late Charles Banks, and the entire Banks family, I cherish the decades of memories from Ashburton Street to Loudon Avenue. You have loved me like a son and brother, and you gave me Ronaé.

Ronaé, you are worthy of an entire acknowledgment. You are the custom (handcrafted) gift that God has given me for life. There is no doubt in my mind that God created you, alone, to minister to me throughout my nine surgeries, drug addictions, two out of body experiences, paralysis, and just too many other dysfunctions to name. Had it not been for you Ronaé, loving me at my worst, I would not be standing today. You have withstood the test of time (thirty-nine years and counting). For you my love, I bow my head in gratitude. I'll spend the rest of my life honoring your commitment to me.

To my daughter Dr. Monaé Raphael who from the age of two, to an adult, has encouraged me. You believed and trusted the God of your parents as a Healer. Furthermore, you have consistently walked me through the process to write my first book. Monaé, thank you and I promise the second book will come soon. And to my son and namesake, Dr. Marcus Aaron Johnson, Jr., who constantly encourages me with the words "Dad you can do it" and "Dad I'm so proud of you." Marcus these words mean the world to me son. I love you and I thank you.

To my editor and lifelong friend, Elder Lois McMillan, M.L.A., Assistant Professor, Morgan State University, thank you for your pen, edits, and instruction. You clarified my ideas. I value your friendship.

"Iron sharpeneth iron; so a man sharpeneth the countenance of his friend." Proverbs 27:17 (KJV) Minister Beverly Johnson, Minister Don Julian Frazier, and Pastor Leon Pinkett, III, you consistently asked me to write *Watch and See*. You urged me to commit to finish as soon as possible. You reminded me that the testimony remains yet untold to so many. You are my iron sharpeners and I thank you.

I honor the memory of the late Chief Apostle Monroe Randolph Saunders, Sr., D.Min., and the life of Lady Alberta Saunders. Under your shepherding I was birthed into sonship, nurtured into discipleship, mentored into the deeper life experience, and launched into ministry as a pastor. Thank you for your selfless tutelage and loving guidance. You soar with eagles' wings.

I honor the memory of the late Dr. Elijah Saunders, my primary care physician and friend. As chief steward of my medical care, you were consistently invested in my well-being for nearly four decades. Even in our final conversation in 2015, you reiterated your passion that all pastors maintain their health. Sir, you were a pioneering leader, clinician, and researcher. I will forever be grateful that you intervened time and time again on my behalf.

I would also like to acknowledge Bishop Monroe Randolph Saunders, Jr., D.Min., Presiding Prelate of the United Church of Jesus Christ, and my Pastor for nearly a decade; Bishop James David Nelson, Sr., Founder and Presiding Prelate Emeritus of the World Assemblies of Restoration, and my spiritual father (succeeding my first); and Bishop Angel Luis Nuñez, M.A., D.Div., Founder and Senior Pastor of the Bilingual Christian Church, and my covenant brother. Thank you for walking with me in my journey.

To Lawyer William Cooper, Dr. David Anderson, Dr. Tony Evans, and Dr. Donna Saunders, your book endorsements came so quickly. I value my relationship with each of you and I admire you.

To my Xlibris Publishing Team (Mary, Clyde, Ryan, Jay, Cheryl, Lani, and your wonderful staff), thank you for your efforts and for treating me like a VIP.

And finally, to my natural family members; my church family the New Harvest Ministries, Inc.; the New Harvest Fellowship of Ministries International; and the many other churches where I have ministered around the world, I acknowledge your innumerable words of encouragement to write this book. Thank you all. May the Lord enrich you to finish your assignments with victory and joy. "Watch and See."

About the Author

Bishop Marcus A. Johnson, Sr. is the Senior Pastor of the New Harvest Ministries, Inc., the Presiding Prelate of the New Harvest Fellowship of Churches, and the CEO of the Bridge to Life Community Development Corporation, Inc., based in Baltimore, Maryland. He also serves as a life coach, motivational speaker, international missionary, and in various capacities bridging the gap between police and communities, generations, races/ethnicities, and faith-based groups. Bishop Johnson champions prayer, reconciliation, unity, and social justice. Standing with him in ministry are his wife, Ronaé, children, and a host of co-laborers. Bishop Johnson is a multifaceted leader with a global vision to reap a kingdom harvest for Christ.

Printed in the United States
By Bookmasters